FORE-
CLOSED

Barry Bergdoll
Reinhold Martin

The Museum of Modern Art, New York
In association with The Temple Hoyne Buell Center for
the Study of American Architecture, Columbia University,
New York

FORE-CLOSED:

REHOUSING THE AMERICAN DREAM

Published in conjunction with the
exhibition *Foreclosed: Rehousing the
American Dream*, organized at The
Museum of Modern Art, New York, by
Barry Bergdoll, The Philip Johnson Chief
Curator of Architecture and Design,
MoMA, with Reinhold Martin, Director,
Temple Hoyne Buell Center for the Study
of American Architecture, Columbia
University. It runs from February 15 to
July 30, 2012

The exhibition is made possible by The
Rockefeller Foundation. This is the
second exhibition in the series Issues in
Contemporary Architecture, supported
by Andre Singer.

The accompanying workshops are made
possible by MoMA's Wallis Annenberg
Fund for Innovation in Contemporary Art
through the Annenberg Foundation.

Additional support for the publication is
provided by The Richard H. Driehaus
Foundation.

Produced by the Department of
Publications, The Museum of Modern Art,
New York

Edited by David Frankel
Designed by MTWTF (Glen Cummings,
Juan Astasio, Aliza Dzik, Andrew Shurtz),
New York
Production by Matthew Pimm
Printed and bound by Asia One Printing
Limited, Hong Kong

This book is typeset in Akzidenz-Grotesk.
The paper is 120gsm White A woodfree

Published by The Museum of Modern Art,
11 W. 53 Street, New York, New York 10019

Library of Congress Control Number:
2012931748
ISBN: 978-0-87070-827-5

Distributed in the United States and
Canada by D.A.P./Distributed Art
Publishers, Inc., New York.
Distributed outside the United States and
Canada by Thames & Hudson Ltd, London.

Secretary Shaun Donovan's speech
and the proceedings of the June 18
workshops were transcribed from audio
recordings into type by CastingWords,
at http://castingwords.com.

Cover, back cover, and flaps: details
of the five *Foreclosed* projects by MOS
Architects, Visible Weather, Studio
Gang Architects, WORKac, and Zago
Architecture.

Printed and bound in Hong Kong

In its promotion of the most pertinent and innovative architecture of the day, The Museum of Modern Art has since its founding given issues of housing and urbanism pride of place alongside aesthetic and formal questions. With the complex and timely project *Foreclosed: Rehousing the American Dream*, we renew that legacy. It is too often forgotten that precisely eighty years ago, the Museum's epoch-making *Modern Architecture: International Exhibition* of 1932 not only promoted the aesthetic principles of what curators Henry-Russell Hitchcock and Philip Johnson saw as an emerging "International Style," but also—with the collaboration of the writer Lewis Mumford—advocated housing reform in the slums of New York and other American cities as the effects of the worldwide economic depression began to make themselves profoundly felt. In recent years that advocacy role has again been a hallmark of our Department of Architecture and Design, particularly in the series "Issues in Contemporary Architecture," which challenges architects to confront problems they don't necessarily face in the direct commissions and design competitions that are the usual vehicles for new design thinking.

The series was inaugurated in 2010, with *Rising Currents: Projects for New York's Waterfront*, which invited a broad range of designers to work together to imagine ways to make cities more resilient to the rising sea levels brought on by climate change. With that project, Barry Bergdoll, the Museum's Philip Johnson Chief Curator of Architecture and Design, also created a unique collaboration between the Museum and its sister institution MoMA PS1, which provided studio space for workshops open to public visits and debates while design was under way. That process was followed by an exhibition of the results at MoMA. In *Foreclosed*, the second project in the series, architects, landscape designers, environmentalists, economists, engineers, community activists, and artists, all practitioners of disciplines that separately and implicitly shape our daily built environment, have come together to think collaboratively and explicitly about new models for future development of suburbs. In an economic climate more and more often compared to that of the Museum's early years in the 1930s, the curators have presented the workshop's design teams with the challenge of seeing a silver lining in the economic downturn—of finding a moment to reflect on the inner ring of suburbs, and on the possibility that they offer the most urgent and most environmentally and often socially sound terrain for rethinking American metropolitan regions in the twenty-first century. Here, in a landscape often leapfrogged over by developers looking for places to build ever farther from the urban core, are fabrics that have the potential to serve a much broader range of the population. In fact the workshop has discovered how diverse the country's suburbs indeed are, and how many opportunities for new types of design engagement reside there.

Foreclosed aims at nothing less than the opposite of its title: to open up new terrain both for building differently and for bringing out-of-the box thinking to bear on the issues that face our extended metropolitan regions. Its innovative methods began with the collaboration between Bergdoll and Professor Reinhold Martin, Director of the Temple Hoyne Buell Center for the Study of American Architecture at Columbia University's Graduate School of Architecture, Planning, and Preservation. I am grateful to them for shepherding this project through its successive stages, each engaging an increasingly broad public in the issues at stake, from the MoMA PS1 workshop and open-house programs, through the website with blog and commentary, to the exhibition at the Museum. I would also like to thank our colleagues at MoMA PS1 for making this experiment possible. Finally, on behalf of the staff and trustees of the Museum, I would like to thank The Rockefeller Foundation, Andre Singer, MoMA's Wallis Annenberg Fund for Innovation in Contemporary Art through the Annenberg Foundation, and The Richard H. Driehaus Foundation, as well as Columbia University's Buell Center, for their indispensable support for the workshop, exhibition, and this publication.

Glenn D. Lowry
Director
The Museum of Modern Art

Preface

The mission of the Buell Center is to advance the interdisciplinary study of American architecture, urbanism, and landscape. As a separately endowed entity affiliated with Columbia University's Graduate School of Architecture, Planning and Preservation, the Center is the only institution of its kind in the United States devoted specifically to the study of American architecture. During the three decades since its formation, in 1982, the Center has sponsored numerous research projects, design workshops, public programs, publications, and awards.

In joining with The Museum of Modern Art to sponsor the workshop whose products are presented in this exhibition, the Buell Center has enlarged the scope of its mission by undertaking first to define an urgent contemporary problem in the built environment and then to participate in the search for innovative solutions. Aside from sharing in the management of *Foreclosed*, the Center's contribution, initiated and led by its director, Reinhold Martin, is embodied in two documents appearing as prologue and afterword to the work presented herein: *The Buell Hypothesis*—the proposition that provoked the endeavor—and a critical essay evaluating the analytic responses and synthetic design proposals received from workshop participants.

The subject of housing and its relationship to concepts of public and private in American society is now at the forefront of our consciousness, yet remains strangely resistant to fruitful discourse as we face the current economic crisis—a crisis in which the calamity of foreclosure has been the most widely felt catalytic episode. The five multidisciplinary teams that accepted our invitation to participate in *Foreclosed* have dared to venture that the imagination of the architect, with essential support from other disciplines, can bring the problem of housing into focus in a way that stimulates the needed discourse and opens it to possibilities that would otherwise remain undiscovered. The Buell Center is full of admiration for the courageous leadership shown by MoMA's Department of Architecture and Design in conceiving and mounting this boldly exploratory exhibition. It has been a privilege for us to participate in thus testing the Buell Hypothesis: "Change the dream and you change the city."

Henry N. Cobb
Chair, Advisory Board
Temple Hoyne Buell Center for the Study of American Architecture

Fig. 1. Levittown, New York, in 1958. Built by the developer William Levitt in Nassau County, Long Island, outside New York City, in 1947–51.

Reopening Foreclosure
Barry Bergdoll

At the age of sixty-five or so, the great American dream of residential suburbia (fig. 1), which came of age with the GI Bill of the 1940s and America's postwar economic and baby booms, seems about ready to retire.[1] Not, however—as it might have been planning—to one of the recently built "communities" of supersized developer houses, each surrounded on its individual lot by a narrow frame of manicured lawn, that in the last decade or so have come to circle the outer fringe of nearly every American city. There, developers churned out readymade dreams on an ever larger scale, producing rings of often monofunctional bulge—carpets here of overscaled houses, there of big-box retail stores—in an all-but-unprecedented building boom fueled by easy credit and binge mortgage practices. Not only are these houses now failing to appeal to buyers, including the young families who moved so dramatically to the suburbs in the 1940s and '50s, but they are also ill adapted to the complex demographics of today's new suburban population and unamenable to conversion to other purposes. Many of these developments—more real estate investments than places—are now, at scarcely a decade old, landscapes of partial abandonment, disinvestment, and foreclosure, symptoms that strikingly recall the malaise of inner-city neighborhoods in the 1960s and early '70s, as postwar "white flight" fueled an earlier generation of suburban growth.[2] Are these landscapes to be left to decay? Or is there a future for a built environment that both absorbed vast resources to create and fueled much of the growth in individual wealth over the last couple of decades, wealth at present in peril with the rolling mortgage crisis, which had already gained steam for several years before the financial crisis of autumn 2008? Is that model of building to be left intact, to be set in operation again on the diminishing supply of undeveloped land if and when the current recession fades into consciousness as a bad dream?

    In the fifteen years leading up to the collapse of the housing market—the first signs that air was escaping from that speculative bubble came in 2006, when the subprime mortgage crisis became evident and the market peaked—a productive discourse on rethinking suburbia arose, largely sponsored by the Congress for the New Urbanism (founded in 1993), with its ethos of densification, walkability, and mixed use (fig. 2), and by the rise of the Smart Growth movement.[3] Yet apart from isolated cases across the country, both of these drives were largely offset by the overheated market for turnkey developments on new exurban sites, which leapfrogged the older suburban-sprawl model of development into virgin territory—the path of least resistance for most developer models. By the height of the housing

Fig. 2. Wellington, Palm Beach County, Florida. A typical New Urbanist plan, designed in 1989 by Duany Plater-Zyberk & Co., Miami.

boom, the average size of the American house had increased by almost 140 percent in just over a half century, from around 983 square feet in 1950 to around 2,349 in 2004 (fig. 3).[4] Almost all open space between cities seemed poised to give birth to neighborhoods of such houses, and these neighborhoods, accessible only by car, were to involve long and, given soaring gasoline prices, increasingly costly commutes to workplaces and shops. This development model was largely impervious to cries of ecological unsustainability, but in the wake of the foreclosure crisis it has run completely out of steam.

Nevertheless, as architect Aron Chang notes in his perceptive recent analysis "Beyond Foreclosure," "The disconnection between the rising diversity of housing needs and the monotony of housing production speaks to the tenacity of the postwar American dream—the enduring allure of the detached house with front lawn and backyard patio—as well as to the profitability of catering to these aspirations."[5] Half of the American population today lives in suburban communities.[6] That population, however, bears little resemblance to the white middle-class average-family composition of postwar television sitcoms, or to the life-style dreams embodied in the house "products" of most suburban developers. Ethnically, racially, and in terms of family composition, twenty-first-century suburbs are often every bit as diverse as cities. In 2010, poverty in suburbs reached its highest level since the U.S. Census Bureau first began to record income statistics, in 1967;[7] and numerous demographic studies have shown that suburbs are aging, as baby boomers stay put there and younger people choose to become urban homesteaders rather than suburban soccer moms.[8] The percentage of households without children is growing nearly as fast in suburbs as in cities, and where newly arrived immigrants once made their first stop in urban tenements they now often go directly to suburbs—or what might once have been called suburbs, I should say; for if one thing is abundantly clear it is that there is scarcely such a thing as a "typical suburb" (fig. 4) anywhere but in the American imaginary. And that imaginary is in a state of shock and anxiety brought on by the collapse of the model of economic growth and abundance that has fueled the American suburban dream for the last sixty-five+ years—by scenes of houses boarded up even in formerly affluent areas, of neighbors in foreclosure, of houses worth less than the outstanding sums on their mortgages.

Foreclosed: Rehousing the American Dream sets out to address this complex national emergency, at once a cause and a symptom of the mortgage-default crisis, on which our project seizes as a rare chance for fresh thinking. While architects, urban and landscape designers, and infrastructure engineers can do little directly about the problem of foreclosed mortgages

Fig. 3. Unidentified "McMansion."

Fig. 4. The house of the Cleaver family in the television sitcom *Leave It to Beaver*, 1957–63. The Cleavers lived here during four of the show's six seasons.

and households "under water" (that being a crisis of the financial architecture of America), they can address the risks of a downward spiral of disinvestment in suburbs. In this sense discussions that have been foreclosed for decades can now again be had, a change potently underscored by *The Buell Hypothesis*, a two-year study, conducted by Columbia University's Temple Hoyne Buell Center for the Study of American Architecture, that maps foreclosures in eight metropolitan regions and is summarized in the present volume. Written by Professor Reinhold Martin, Leah Meisterlin, Anna Kenoff, and a group of doctoral students in urban planning at Columbia University, *The Buell Hypothesis* also invites a reconsideration of the residential landscape of suburbia and of the public and private values that build it and are preserved there. The questions involved are not limited to the market's supply of housing types that do not correspond to our society's diverse needs and are not adaptable to change, or to the role that zoning, restrictive covenants, and home-owners'-association regulations often place on occupancy, mixed use, and even issues of density. All of these are factors not only in the unsustainable landscape of single uses—tracts of housing separated by miles from the nearest convenience store, for instance—but also in the creation of a landscape remarkably inflexible to the plate tectonics of global capital in an era of abstract financial instruments.

Beyond such questions, *The Buell Hypothesis* (fig. 5)—which the Buell Center self-published and MoMA made available as a research report to the architect-led teams that designed projects for *Foreclosed*—proposes a new national discussion about the relationship between the public and the private, a relationship blurred in a period when "public/private partnerships" involving the sale of public land to private developers in deals intended to produce affordable housing, or the restructuring of what used to be public services and utilities in market terms, have become common political and financial devices. After two generations of privatization of everything from public housing to public space, and the invention of ever more complex forms of public/private partnership, many Americans have begun to question a whole series of previously unexamined assumptions. Home ownership—long promoted by federal mortgage subsidies, highway building programs, and numerous other incentives—is now seen as anything but a universal panacea. Besides the issue of affordability (rendered more and more problematic with the scaling back of federal programs such as Hope VI, which often improved the quality of public housing but also often reduced the supply of affordable homes within given areas), it is apparent that in a severely diminished job market, home ownership brings with it a lack of mobility and flexibility. Even while the plans for high-speed rail corridors that President Barack Obama announced in 2009, as part

Fig. 5. *The Buell Hypothesis*, published by the Temple Hoyne Buell Center for the Study of American Architecture, Columbia University, in 2011.

of the national stimulus package, have suffered huge setbacks, there is a new receptiveness to discussions of altering the "natural" regime of the car, now that soaring gasoline prices are straining many household budgets. The rise of both the Tea Party and the Occupy Wall Street movement since the onset of the current fiscal crisis and economic downturn shows that more and more citizens want a broader discussion of the nature and parameters of the American Dream.

In the America that will emerge from the great recession of the early twenty-first century, the unrolling of a welcome mat to developers across the landscape is in all likelihood endangered, unsustainable ecologically, demographically, economically, socially, and probably even politically. No Noah's ark can be constructed to preserve existing species of urban and suburban development through the present deluge, over the roofs as it were of underwater properties. Instead, as Andrew Zago's project for Rialto, California, polemically asserts, the moment demands enormous hybridization and the development of basically new species of designed environments, in which uses, demographics, and ownership models have been rethought, reinvigorated, and given new resilience, essentially crafting new individual and collective ways of living. In all likelihood, new modes of ownership will emerge, not merely new financial "products" to be bought and sold in global markets but experiments with different individual and collective ownership assumptions.

Foreclosed: Rehousing the American Dream follows a model set at MoMA in 2010 by the *Rising Currents* project, in which the Museum paired five interdisciplinary teams—each assembled by one or more emerging designers, of great talent and vision, as team leaders— with five different sites in New York Harbor to create ideas for alternative futures in response to a pressing issue: climate change, and in particular rising sea levels and more-frequent storm surges. The five teams' design studio at MoMA PS1, the Museum's affiliate in Long Island City, Queens, became a public forum, and the results of their work were exhibited at the Museum (fig. 6), published, and debated on the MoMA website.[9] New conversations were begun not only with city officials but also with city residents and with architects and architecture students. Although *Rising Currents* faced a problem that is ultimately global, its focus was local; *Foreclosed*, on the other hand, addresses an issue at a national scale.

As in *Rising Currents*, the five *Foreclosed* teams began, not with a specific brief, but with a major body of research brought together in *The Buell Hypothesis*, a strong statement to which to respond and react. This time the sites were not familiar parts of the shoreline of New York City and adjacent New Jersey, all visible from the Verrazano-Narrows Bridge, the Staten Island Ferry,

Fig. 6. *Rising Currents: Projects for New York's Waterfront.* Installation view of the exhibition at The Museum of Modern Art, New York, March 24–October 11, 2010.

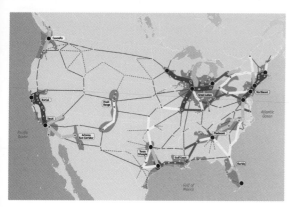

Fig. 7. A phasing plan for high-speed rail corridors in the United States, as proposed by the America2050 initiative of the Regional Plan Association.

or from many of the planes that land at Newark, JFK, and LaGuardia airports. Instead they were suburban municipalities, often unknown to almost everyone but those who live or work there or nearby (although anyone who buys mail-order goods from Staples, for instance, has probably received packages from Rialto). These sites were "unearthed" through multicriteria analyses that yielded a set of suburbs with shared characteristics across the country: all are set within a major corridor between two cities that are projected to add population in coming decades. All lie on or near one of the projected high-speed rail lines discussed in the more hopeful days of 2009, when this form of transportation, which rewrote the economy of Europe in the late twentieth century and is now doing the same in China, was thought possible at least on a limited basis in the United States (fig. 7; much of course would depend on the placement of stations and nodal points on those lines). Most important, all have experienced high rates of foreclosure, and continue to shelter many properties at risk of foreclosure; and in addition to their properties now held by banks—some of which are themselves only above water because of federal bailout moneys—as of February 2009 (the date of the American Recovery and Reinvestment Act, and of the statistics gathered for the project) all contained sizable tracts of publicly owned lands, sites potentially available for public/private initiatives that could test new design ideas. In several cases public/private deals have already been struck for these lands, and in some a master plan along New Urbanist principles is in the works. The aim of *Foreclosed* is not, as in New Urbanism, to apply a type of "code-based urbanism" that largely accepts zoning restrictions and tax codes as they are written—a kind of pragmatism sometimes dressed up with nostalgia—but rather to challenge the status quo and devise workable new models that imply different ways of living, legislating, and financing. The aim is to provide the elements for a wide-open discussion of the look of the expanded American metropolis, and of its political and financial underpinnings, in the twenty-first century.

Under the leadership of five architectural practices that are among the most innovative in the country today, the teams were tasked with generating new ideas from a back-and-forth exploration of urban and architectural solutions and with imagining new financial architectures to create viable and vibrant new places on existing sites. Each team included members with expertise in economics, finance, housing, and public policy. In addition, some teams included ecologists, landscape designers, or community organizers, who offered ideas for postulating a brief and its physical manifestation in forms rarely possible in private-sector architectural offices. Setting out to provide designers with a wholly new frame for thinking about the issues, we tested their ideas against the reactions of visiting experts and members of the public, working with both closed weekly pin-up sessions and open houses whose attendees ranged from MoMA PS1's neighbors in Long Island City to the U.S. Secretary of Housing and Urban Development (HUD), Shaun Donovan. The designers fielded and received feedback on their ideas, and the public had the opportunity to see that design is a way of thinking, not simply a way of prettifying decisions that are made in other arenas (figs. 8–11).

In the early weeks, in May and June 2011, the teams set out to make themselves at home in the suburbs analyzed in *The Buell Hypothesis*, visiting potential sites for intervention, meeting with local residents and in some cases with local officials, and considering what type of architectural program would respond to local needs and the realities of the existing population rather than the market share of a future population. We quickly learned that the five chosen areas (along with three others discussed in *The Buell Hypothesis* that the project could not include) were in fact radically different from one another, even though each seemed highly familiar and in many important senses might stand in for the others. These areas, all of which might be called "suburbs," run the gamut from places immediately outside the boundaries of older cities—Orange, New Jersey (fig. 12), for example, outside both New York City and Newark, or Cicero, Illinois (fig. 13), outside Chicago—to a recent failed developer subdivision on the unincorporated edge of Rialto (fig. 14), nearly a two-hour drive from downtown Los Angeles (in rush hour). While vastly different, all feature housing stock that bears little relationship to the demands of a broad swath of the market for housing in their respective regions. In Orange and Cicero, the houses in question are largely bungalows and other older, modestly scaled single-family structures, whose residents, overwhelmingly new immigrants, must seek ingenious retrofits to accommodate multigenerational arrangements and often need to break zoning codes to mix residential and commercial functions. The failed subdivision in Rialto meanwhile contains houses whose square footage is inflated to the point where they seem almost to rub against one another, although the landscape is vast and open, and just as in Orange, there is a misfit between the diversity of the residents of this part of the San Bernardino Valley and the narrow range of housing "products" on offer. Also, in that the subdivision was intended as a bedroom commuting community, it principally addresses the interstate, having little relationship to Rialto's downtown or to regional rail services. Both Temple Terrace, Florida (fig. 15), and Keizer, Oregon (fig. 16), are older suburbs whose edges could be redefined in ways that would be transformative not only for the municipality but for the larger region, and that might be paradigmatic far beyond it. In all cases development and transportation are poorly coordinated, and existing

Figs. 8–11. Top to bottom: *Foreclosed* orientation, May 2011, MoMA PS1, Long Island City. MOS *Foreclosed* workshop, MoMA PS1. Andrew Zago presenting his project for Rialto at the *Foreclosed* open house at MoMA PS1, June 2011. Final open house at MoMA PS1, September 2011, with Michael Bell of Visible Weather explaining his project for Temple Terrace, Florida, to Secretary of Housing and Urban Development Shaun Donovan.

Figs. 12, 13 (below), 14–16. Top to bottom: site research photographs by team members showing views of Orange, New Jersey; Cicero, Illinois; Rialto, California; Temple Terrace, Florida; and Keizer, Oregon.

public transportation is underexploited and is discussed and funded in a completely different arena. Although HUD has begun to discuss a more integrated approach to development in its various programs, these are underfunded, few and far between, and have no spillover into the private sector.

The five projects that emerged from the workshops, as well as the discussions, presentations, and debates that guided them and that they in turn engendered, are brought together in this book. They provide radically different visions of a rethought suburbia, ones in which the very notion of suburbia is transformed. As such they represent an expansion of the palette of thinking laid out in Ellen Dunham-Jones and June Williamson's New Urbanist *Retrofitting Suburbia*, pragmatic and considered though that book is—a veritable manual for thinking about how to make suburbia work within the parameters of existing codes and financial instruments, it was presented to the teams at the outset of the project as a set of existing options.[10] None of the solutions is mutually exclusive, none a blueprint for building that could be sent out for bid tomorrow. Rather, the projects together constitute an invitation for new approaches, further research, and the creation of places incorporating greater sustainability, better transportation, more flexible housing, and neighborhoods that are both individually and collectively appealing as imagined daily environments.

Each project seeks to break down the inherited strictures that are often enshrined in building codes but no longer work for large parts of the American population, such as the segregation through zoning of residential areas, commercial activity, and production, or restrictions on the mix of generations within a single household through the creation of separate "grandmother" apartments. Just as around 1900 the Garden City movement sought to combine the benefits of city and country into a new form of urban living, so today, when downtowns are being remade by parks and recreation zones, and when districts are being rezoned to mix functions in ways that were unthinkable in a past of heavy industry, it is time to recognize that suburbs can be reinvigorated by new approaches to living and to ownership. Thus Visible Weather, working with Jesse Keenan, has developed a novel form of Real Estate Investment Trust (REIT) to question the current tendency to transfer ownership of land from taxpayers to private developers. Working with the economist Edward Glaeser, MOS proposes a Limited Equity Company to hold ownership of streets converted into buildings in the rail core of Orange, these new linear structures mixing scales, uses, and spatial experiences in unprecedented ways. In "Garden in the Machine," the team led by Studio Gang proposes a radical division between land ownership and unit ownership in which residents can buy and sell space as needed to create a flexible system of dwelling, at the same time preserving equity—in both financial and social terms—and a sense of civic belonging.

Like many recent artistic projects that have made the extent of foreclosure visible and given a focus to the suffering and hardship it creates—one thinks of Damon Rich's *Red Lines Housing Crisis Learning Center* of 2008 (fig. 17) and of Keller Easterling's *Takeaway*, among the most pointed artistic expressions of the challenge to the American dream—the projects here are meant to open our minds to new thinking more than they are to be taken as literal blueprints.[11] Little of what is proposed in this volume can be built today, not because it exceeds our technological capacities, as some earlier visionary projects did (the glass skyscrapers of Mies van der Rohe, for example, in the 1920s), but merely because it demands a willingness to reenvision not only the types of places we build but the way that we own and administer them. Many break down the notion that the individual object—the single house as an architectural design, a home, or the building block of a community—is the sine qua non of our shared desires. Some even return to large-scale structures that presuppose substantial upfront investment but in return create not only new types of dwelling but also renewed possibilities for civic and quotidian interaction. The ideal of the New England town need not manifest itself in the neocolonial house; indeed few have proposed as radical a return to the town meeting as Visible Weather does in its layered tensegrity structure, which places an invisible city hall at the heart of a mixed-used community—a notion of civic administration as ubiquitous rather than monumentalized. Meanwhile Studio Gang has developed a flexible model of dwelling that is adaptable to a family's changing needs and budget rather than acting as a commodity to be bought and sold like a stock option. In the end, the proposals here are every bit as pragmatic as many developer-friendly solutions, whether those of the conventional type or those framed in New Urbanist modes. They simply demand that we be willing to change the codes that produce a (sub)urbanism that is no longer sustainable, or even, it seems, able to find the market share it was calculated to enchant.

1. For an overview of the development of the American suburb see Kenneth Jackson, *Crabgrass Frontier: The Suburbanization of the United States* (New York: Oxford University Press, 1985), and more recently Dolores Hayden, *Building Suburbia: Green Fields and Urban Growth, 1820–2000* (New York: Vintage Books, 2003).

2. See, e.g., the documentation by the photographer David Wells, "Foreclosed Dreams," online at http://www.davidhwells.com/docuForeclosedDreams/index.html#_self.

3. See in particular Ellen Dunham-Jones and June Williamson, *Retrofitting Suburbia: Urban Design Solutions for Redesigning Suburbs* (New York: Wiley & Sons, 2008).

4. See Sarah Z. Wexler, *Living Large: From SUVs to Double Ds, Why Going Bigger Isn't Going Better* (New York: St. Martin's Press, 2010), p. 14, or e.g., http://realestate.msn.com/article.aspx?cp-documentid=13107733.

5. Aron Chang, "Beyond Foreclosure: The Future of Suburban Housing," in *Design Observer: Places*, September 14, 2011, online at http://places.designobserver.com/feature/beyond-foreclosure-the-future-of-suburban-housing/29438/.

6. See Frank Hobbs and Nicole Stoops, *Demographic Trends in the 20th Century*, U.S. Census Bureau, Census 2000 Special Reports, Series CENSR-4 (Washington, D.C.: U.S. Government Printing Office, 2002), p. 33. Available online at http://www.census.gov/prod/2002pubs/censr-4.pdf.

7. See Jason DeParle and Sabrina Tavernise, "Poor Are Still Getting Poorer, but Downturn's Punch Varies, Census Data Show," *New York Times*, September 15, 2011, p. A25.

8. See William H. Frey, "The Great American Migration Slowdown: Regional and Metropolitan Dimensions" (Washington, D.C.: Metropolitan Policy Program, Brookings Institute, December 2009), online at http://www.brookings.edu/~/media/Files/rc/reports/2009/1209_migration_frey/1209_migration_frey.pdf.

9. Online at http://www.moma.org/explore/inside_out/category/rising-currents. See also Barry Bergdoll, *Rising Currents: Projects for New York's Waterfront* (New York: The Museum of Modern Art, 2011), and Bergdoll, "The Art of Advocacy: The Museum as Design Laboratory," *Design Observer: Places*, September 16, 2011, online at http://places.designobserver.com/feature/the-art-of-advocacy-moma-as-design-laboratory/29638/.

10. Dunham-Jones and Williamson's book served in part as the inspiration for the "Build a Better Burb" competition on Long Island in 2009–10. See http://buildabetterburb.org.

11. Keller Easterling's project was first published as "Architecture to Take Away," in Ilka and Andreas Ruby, eds., *Re-inventing Construction* (Berlin: Ruby Press, 2010), pp. 265–74. A refined version is forthcoming in *Perspecta 45: Agency*, Fall 2012.

Fig. 17. Damon Rich. *Cities Destroyed for Cash*, part of the exhibition *Red Lines Housing Crisis Learning Center*, 2009. 1,431 plastic markers on the Panorama of the City of New York, Queens Museum of Art. Commissioned by the Queens Museum of Art. Courtesy the artist and the Queens Museum of Art. With assistance from Rana Amirtahmasebi, the Neighborhood Economic Development Advocacy Project, and the Regional Plan Association.

THE BUELL HYPOTHESIS

Reinhold Martin, Leah Meisterlin, and Anna Kenoff

In 2009, the Temple Hoyne Buell Center for the Study of American Architecture at Columbia University issued the pamphlet "Public Housing: A New Conversation." The aim of this small volume was to respond to the ongoing mortgage-foreclosure crisis, not with narrow solutions but with a broad reformulation of the problem; one that could encourage a different kind of public conversation about housing and, by extension, about cities.

The Buell Hypothesis follows up on that initiative. The result of three years of work by an interdisciplinary team of researchers, it translates technical analysis into cultural terms, to show how the assumptions underlying urban and economic policies and practices in the United States might be changed. The first section unfolds an argument about housing in the American suburbs as a matter of public concern. The second section (omitted here) excerpts public debates about housing and cities from the early twentieth century to the present, and profiles selected architectural projects on which such debates have centered. The third section outlines a series of contexts in which to test or to revise the argument's premises with concrete propositions that might become the basis for a renewed debate.

The hypothesis therefore reframes the question of housing—and, in particular, the single-family suburban house—as a question of publicly negotiable cultural values. This means treating seemingly straightforward technical facts, from demographic trends to environmental impacts, as partly conditioned by narratives, or stories, that convert those negotiable values into apparent truths.

One such story, commonly told, is known as the "American Dream." There is no set unfolding to this story; nor are its most recognizable characteristics uniquely American. Its unifying, recurring theme, however, is the idea that full participation in civic and social life is premised on homeownership, whether literal or symbolic. This theme corresponds with the centrality of the single-family house in defining settlement patterns throughout the United States, particularly in suburban and exurban areas. For more than a century, these patterns and their underlying story have been reinforced by zoning codes, housing policies, construction techniques, architectural designs, and, as the 2008 economic crisis showed, increasingly elaborate financial instruments.

The Buell Hypothesis, at its most basic, argues as follows: change the dream and you change the city. The single-family house and the city or suburb in which it is situated share a common destiny. Hence, change the narratives guiding suburban housing and the priorities they imply, including spatial arrangements, ownership patterns, the balance between public and private interests, and the mixtures of activities and services that any town or city entails, and you begin the process of redirecting suburban sprawl.

To exemplify the narrative character of knowledge that informs architecture, urbanism, and the policies that guide them, we have chosen to present this hypothesis in the form of a screenplay. We treat the American Dream metaphorically as a film with a familiar plot, characters, and setting. In order to explore its assumptions, we overlay it with another story, a road movie, wherein house and suburb serve as props in a philosophical conversation about basic human priorities as expressed, in this case, through ways of living. The action is set at a potential turning point: February 18, 2009, the day after U.S. President Barack Obama signed the American Recovery and Reinvestment Act (ARRA). The conversation takes the form of a latter-day Socratic dialogue and symposium, with characters borrowed from ancient Athens. In adapting this genre, which emphasizes informed debate over unexamined dogma, we aim to prompt the type of serious, reflective conversation that occurs after viewing a thought-provoking film, the kind that begins in cinema lobbies and parking lots, continues into cars, restaurants, and living rooms, and eventually enters newspapers, blogs, and social media.

This, among other things, is what it might mean to discuss the architecture of housing and of the American suburbs in public. As shown by the historical material integrated into our story, debates about housing and cities have in fact been an important part of the public conversation for nearly 100 years. Today, these debates have narrowed in their terms: they have often taken for granted recent developments like the suburban house and its environs, while accepting a severely limited role for public or civic interests in housing policy and practice. Reactivating and broadening such debates suggests a variety of not-yet-imagined but entirely realistic alternatives to current practices. More than simply providing technical solutions, these alternatives could give new meaning to ideas such as "house," "home," and "city." Toward this end, the original document included a series of representative case studies featuring municipalities across the country where the need for inclusive housing models is particularly acute. These are summarized below. Each offers a somewhat different context in which our hypothesis might be tested. They synthesize demographics, urban geography, and public policy in a way that expands on the opportunity to tell a different story. In that sense, this film is both documentary and imaginary. It describes a world in which fiction informs fact just as much as fact informs fiction. This is the world we share. We hope that you will enjoy it.

FADE IN

MONTAGE – MID-AFTERNOON
An empty living room with the television on
A cul-de-sac of single-family homes in a suburban subdivision
A group of subdivisions forming a suburb
A cluster of suburbs forming a region

NARRATOR [VOICE-OVER]
This is a story about the way we live today. It is about how we imagine the way we live, about how we represent that to ourselves, about how we feel about those representations, and about how we act on them. It describes these processes as they apply to cities and, in particular, to what we call the "American suburbs." There, as elsewhere, the question of housing is located at the crossroads of economics, public policy, social relations, and culture, with architecture at its very center. The story begins in the present, a time of foreclosure in multiple senses of the term, but it also revisits the debates of the past and anticipates a more open future.

We are often told that human happiness has coexisted with social and environmental equity only in times gone by. This sentiment is especially common when artistic beauty is added to the mix as the bearer of transcendent human feeling. When it comes to cities, towns, and rural settlements, these bygone times are so distant and so idealized that they are for all practical purposes inaccessible, which further enhances their aura as objects of a very potent and, strangely, very future-oriented longing. In contrast, the recent past (which in our case is the past of architectural modernism) is dwelt upon more for its failures than for its achievements. The result is a strong sense of dead ends and misguided ambitions. This is especially true when it comes to housing and its attendant urbanism. Innovation in this area remains one of modernism's principal contributions, and yet modern architecture has long been held responsible for the failure of many efforts to house the world's population.[1] Seen in this way, the integral relation between housing and

21   The Buell Hypothesis

urbanism has led to much concern about what is wrong with modern cities and with the ambitions they harbor.

Such is the state of urbanism today. Its dominant tone is one of regret. There is the overwhelming sense of a lost classical or rural past, of an Arcadia once dotted with small towns, now overrun with suburban subdivisions. And there is the equally overwhelming and equally regretful sense of an onrushing future: a sprawling urbanity of automobiles, highways, big-box stores, gated communities, and the arcane financial instruments that support them. The managers of this new frontier may be, among others, derivatives traders, real estate investors, and hedge-fund executives, but the future on which they trade is shaped by architects, urban planners, landscape architects, engineers, sociologists, geographers, demographers, politicians, and philosophers.

Philosophers? Yes, since philosophy has always concerned itself with stories about logical possibilities and hence about possible futures. Among these, stories about ideal and not-so-ideal cities abound. We have all heard versions of such stories, although we are unlikely to have assumed they had any actual bearing on future cities and suburbs—that is, on the real world of facts and figures, maps and charts, bricks and mortar, dollars and dividends. And yet, listen to any land speculator, real estate investor, banker, bond trader, or market analyst reflect on the future upon which they are betting and you will hear something resembling a philosophy.

This philosophical terrain is what architects call a "site." That it exists in the minds of citizens, politicians, clients, or simply inhabitants of ordinary cities and towns makes it no less real than more conventional sites, with their seemingly more certain terrain of contours, climate, and delineated boundaries. The same can be said for what architects usually call "program," or "use," or "function." For whatever philosophy informs a particular work of architecture, or whatever pragmatic decisions the work entails, the actual lives lived within its walls can never be summarized with shorthand terms like "commercial," "institutional," "recreational," or "residential." What, after all, is "residential" life? "Commercial" life? "Recreation"? We think we understand intuitively what these terms mean, but we also understand that they function as metaphors—as useful approximations that help planners, architects, and other professionals to design for the complex activities they expect will occur in a given place. In this respect, there is no architectural metaphor more elusive than housing, especially as regards the single-family house and its rooms. What, after all, is a "living" room? And even if we could define it, how would we distinguish the acts of living that take place there from those that occur in other rooms, such as the bedroom? How many movies, television shows, and YouTube videos—domestic dramas, comedies, thrillers, and mysteries—have been made to explore poetically, with humor, empathy, and insight, the actual activities that occur in actual houses?

MONTAGE — LATE AFTERNOON
An empty living room with the television on
A cul-de-sac of single-family homes in a suburban subdivision
A group of subdivisions forming a suburb
A cluster of suburbs forming a region

NARRATOR [VOICE-OVER]
The metaphor of housing, or of the house, has decisive practical consequences that continue to reverberate through today's financial markets. Hence the double sense of the word "foreclosure." On the one hand, it is a financial term denoting the termination of a residential mortgage loan that has gone into default; on the other hand, it can signal the closing down of possibilities, the end of a dream. A reality check, perhaps, but also an imperative: don't overreach. There is a long philosophical tradition that asks us to tend our own gardens, to be satisfied with what we have; one that cautions us to avoid impossible utopian idealizations. The arrival of foreclosure signs in suburban cul-de-sacs around the country can be interpreted as a reminder to heed these sensible maxims. To do so, however, would not only confirm the hidden, quasi-philosophical moralism of the financial markets as they slap us on the wrist, it would also misrecognize individual aspiration as collective or societal aspiration. Still, it is possible to say that for many, if not for all, what is frequently called the American Dream was foreclosed upon in 2008.

But what is, or was, this dream? The conquering of frontiers? Self-determination? Homeownership as the mark of independence? What about the collective effort that it takes, even within a family, to own and maintain a home, to say nothing of the tax subsidies and other public expenses dedicated to home mortgages, or the construction and maintenance of roads and other public infrastructures that support any individual house? In this and many other respects, the sense of independence that has defined the American Dream is just as metaphorical as the idea of a universal, all-purpose "house" and its designated rooms for living. Even—or especially—when we own our homes, we continue to depend upon others: others who may or may not share our dreams.

MONTAGE — EARLY EVENING
An empty living room with the television on
A cul-de-sac of single-family homes in a suburban subdivision
A group of subdivisions forming a suburb
A cluster of suburbs forming a region

NARRATOR [VOICE-OVER]
This, too, has philosophical as well as artistic, social, and

economic implications. For it suggests that "home" in the fullest sense is a function of sharing the world with others, including others whom we might not imagine belonging in our own homes. For the American Dream is not a private dream but a public one, financed by tax dollars and played out on national television. Another name for the space in which this dream is formed is the public sphere. This, too, is a site for architecture and urbanism. Throughout the twentieth century, housing has been a central matter of public concern. With the foreclosure crisis, it has returned to join suburban sprawl and environmental devastation as challenges for the twenty-first century. The public sphere in which such matters arise is ideally a space of dialogue and debate, a time-honored practice that also runs through the core of Western philosophy (and of Western democracy, which is not necessarily the same thing). The archetype for this sort of philosophical debate is the Socratic dialogue, which since classical times has taken place in the shadow of architecture.

MONTAGE — DUSK
An empty living room with the television on
A cul-de-sac of single-family homes in a suburban subdivision
A group of subdivisions forming a suburb
A cluster of suburbs forming a region

NARRATOR [VOICE-OVER]
Thus, having finally convinced his pupil (and Plato's older brother) Glaucon of the logical possibility of absolute and true justice administered in the *kallipolis* or ideal city, which is protected by appropriately educated guardians and governed by philosopher-kings, we meet Socrates on the road again, nearly 2½ millennia later.[2] The date is February 18, 2009, and the road is Interstate 95, on the East Coast of the United States. Socrates and Glaucon are stuck in traffic several miles north of exit 160B, which will take them in the direction of Athens, home of the University of Georgia. Socrates has been invited by his former teacher Diotima to speak in a symposium on housing and the American suburbs. Glaucon is at the wheel, and Socrates is in a distinctly un-Platonic state of mind.

Globalization on the Inside

INT. CAR INTERSTATE 95 — MIDDAY
The car carrying SOCRATES and GLAUCON passes Exit 164. Signs pointing in one direction to a Hampton Inn, a Wyndham Inn, a Days Inn, and a Ramada Inn, and in the other direction to downtown Florence and the Florence Regional Airport, line the exit ramp. The Magnolia Mall Shopping Center has not yet come into view on the left. The radio is tuned to talk radio and the talk centers on immigration. Socrates switches the station to National Public Radio. The word "globalization" is heard repeatedly.

GLAUCON
Globalization can only mean one of two things. Either the world is flat: consumerism continues to expand outward from the world's financial centers, the magic of technological networks connects everyone to everyone else, and the free movement of people and ideas across borders makes every city and every suburb that much more multicultural. Or, the world is fortified: the movement of people and ideas across borders threatens national security and hence must be controlled, cheap labor "over there" threatens jobs "over here," and immigration disrupts social equilibrium.

SOCRATES
While both of these perceptions are common, neither is completely accurate. Globalization does not mean "development"; nor does it mean "dissolution." It is a way of thinking about the world. When we say "globalization" we should ask ourselves, "What is being globalized?" Should not the first answer always be "ourselves," even if we never leave home, and even if what we think of as home—a house, a town, a country—seems not to have changed at all?

GLAUCON
But haven't you heard of a "global city"?

SOCRATES
My friend, rather than presupposing that some cities are more "global" than others, you must learn to think about

globalization as an internal process as well as an external one. As it is most commonly used, the term "global city" still suggests a sense of moving outward from an implied center, which is usually located somewhere in Europe or North America, or perhaps in East Asia.

GLAUCON
So?

SOCRATES
For many in the United States, globalization seems to be something that is happening in the world out there, but actually what we are calling globalization begins inside, at home. The mortgage-foreclosure crisis that was intertwined with the financial crisis of 2008 made this clear. Homeowners, and aspiring homeowners, became aware that their sense of "home" was what we might call a "house of cards." Financial ownership of one's dwelling and, with it, a psychological sense of ownership, or rootedness, was shown to be an illusion of sorts, as mortgages were bundled, sold, and resold in markets around the world. This speculative process in turn drove home prices and their associated mortgages to unsustainable levels, even in the most prosperous of communities. The markets collapsed, threatening to bring the major financial institutions down with them. Government intervention was requested—and granted—to shore the whole thing up. In the case of housing, this meant absorbing risk by buying up "distressed" mortgages and offering subsidized (though still market-based) alternatives to the existing mortgage options. It was like rescuing the housing markets by propping up the house of cards with more cards.

GLAUCON
But why do you say that globalization begins at home? As far as I can see, all of the processes that you describe are taking place outside, in the agora or in the marketplace.

SOCRATES
Yes, but in order to work, they rely on an idea of "home"—the one that you hold inside your head, so to speak. In our simplified description of the international financial markets, homeownership, and the *concomitant idea* of "home," are bought and sold, usually with the help of government programs like tax deductions. This demonstrates the connection between the real world of numbers and the equally real world of images, thoughts, and feelings. For despite what you may have heard, we do not live in a cave. In fact, in this country there is a term for the place in which we live. It is called the American Dream.

GLAUCON

The American Dream? You just said that we do not live in a cave.

SOCRATES

That's right.

GLAUCON

I took that to mean that we live in a world more real than the world of shadows and illusions that we might see when we face inward, turning our backs on higher truths. But what is real about a dream?

SOCRATES

The American Dream is as real as any tax deduction, in that it, too, drives the housing markets. Consider a typical suburb, which represents a way of living much more insular but also much more ubiquitous than anything resembling our hypothetical Athenian "republic." The underlying philosophy of homeownership is quite real; that suburb is organized around an ethos that construes homeownership, or at least the feeling of being at home, as something essential or fundamental. But many people also believe that the American Dream represents a specifically "American" way of dreaming, which is fundamentally different from the way others elsewhere in the world might dream. This may be a myth, or merely a culturally reinforced half-truth.... Either way, public policy tends to support it. However, the financial crisis has made clear that the houses in and through which many Americans dream their dreams are not owned by them but rather by banks, whose octopus-like networks make a mockery of national borders, never mind national "dreams." So if the American Dream is a fiction, but a real one—let's say it's a kind of movie—it is a profitable but also a risky one, requiring tax incentives and other types of government support to prop it up and to keep it running in theaters nationwide.

GLAUCON

Socrates, you sounded a bit sarcastic there.

SOCRATES

Really? I did not intend to. Emphasizing its actual, social character rather than its supposed essence, or *mystique*, means considering the American Dream not as a birthright but as one possible dream among many. Though this may seem obvious to some, it is surprising how frequently homeownership is still equated with civic participation.

Can you imagine a situation in which one's home (whether it is owned or rented) is just one commodity among many, comparable to one's car, or computer, or kitchen appliances? No tax breaks, no housing subsidies, no special mortgage programs. In this scenario the house is no longer a special type of commodity, the value of which must be protected at all costs.

GLAUCON
Difficult to imagine, I admit.

SOCRATES
What this scenario brings to light is that in our society (as in most), basic housing is tacitly regarded as something closer to a right than a commodity, or a luxury, or a privilege. Imagine a city overrun with homeless men, women, and children. This is typically interpreted as evidence of societal failure. For in order for any society to be able to imagine itself *as a society*, it must be able to believe itself capable of adequately caring for its constituents. In this case, "adequately cared for" means "adequately housed." How this is to be achieved—whether, say, through the markets or through governmental assistance—might remain a matter of political debate, but that it is to be achieved, one way or the other, cannot be argued.
Financial speculation in real estate, and especially in housing, not only exploits this basic fact, it *requires* it. That is why the American Dream has been such an effective marketing device: it reproduces the illusion that society takes care of its members by affording them the opportunity to take care of themselves, primarily by owning a home. With a home comes a sense of independence.

GLAUCON
I was about to ask what all of this had to do with globalization, but I think I'm beginning to see where you're going. I can see, for example, that it is nonsensical to describe a globalized world simply as either flat or fortified, since the idea of a well-appointed suburban "home"—a house, two cars, a yard with a fence, a stable mortgage—turns out to be one of the main ingredients passing through the circuits of global finance, at least as far as the residential real estate market is concerned. But as you said yourself, this does not necessarily make it illusory or unreal. Why can't I simply accept this idea of "home" and all that it implies—safety, security, family, order—as a simple truth that the market has merely recognized?

SOCRATES
You may, Glaucon, but at your own peril. For to accept this invention as an unquestioned truth is to make the world both flat and fortified at once: flat in terms of the movement of money to and from those who already have it, and fortified in terms of the movement of ideas. Since the most important thing about this idea of "home" is that it does not change; it remains in place, fixed to the ground, even as the dollars passing through

it are converted into credit default swaps and traded in yuan in Shanghai. And an idea that does not change can hardly be called an idea, only a belief.

GLAUCON

But what's wrong with following one's beliefs? What science calls a fact is just as debatable. Sometimes you just have to go with what you believe. And I still believe in the American Dream.

SOCRATES

Well, let's look at it from another direction. Here, Glaucon, is a fact. Did you know that well over one third of the land in the continental United States is owned by the public sector? Much of this is in the form of national parks, military bases, weapons testing ranges, and other large, unbuilt areas. Much is also infrastructural: airports, highway and train right-of-ways, waterfronts, and so on. Even at a much smaller scale, a certain percentage of the land in any township is owned by municipalities or by state or local governments.[3] That means that, theoretically at least, it belongs to all of us.

Yet especially in suburban areas, the dominant impression is that we are looking mainly at private property rather than at public land. This may or may not actually be true for any given vista, but we imagine it to be true. One reason is that Americans have been re-telling the story of the conquest of frontiers since the eighteenth century. This story runs in theaters alongside the American Dream as a kind of double feature. The existence of national parks is partly due to an attempt to preserve this sense of a frontier at the very moment that national expansion had reached certain natural limits. And although public land can therefore represent an imagined frontier for future investment, it also consti-tutes an often invisible, alternative landscape within the dominant landscape of private property in any city, town, or subdivision.

Today, as the actual frontiers of economic expan-sion have moved well beyond the borders of any single country, the old divide between country and city has also been made planetary. The Global South now serves as an agricultural basin for the industrialized North. And yet, in suburbs across the United States, there remains a desire to feel that one is living in the bucolic countryside, even if that countryside is reduced to a patch of lawn and a few trees (not likely elms) along Elm Street. To attract development, municipalities everywhere have drawn up plans that reproduce this bucolic feeling, while identify-ing large and small pieces of land (whether publicly or privately owned) as "investment opportunities." None of this, including the actual visions dreamed up for these sites by architects, planners, and real estate develop-ers, would be conceivable without the pressures, promises, and credit ratings that accompany financial globalization, coupled with the mistaken notion that the public sector has a greatly diminished role to play in imagining the future.

Suburbs Are Cities

INT. CAR INTERSTATE 95 — LATER THAT AFTERNOON
Socrates and Glaucon are still stuck in traffic. The talk on the radio turns to war.

GLAUCON
Speaking of globalization, I keep hearing that half the world's population now lives in cities. Does this have anything to do with how people live here? All I see along this highway is suburban sprawl.[4]

SOCRATES
The United Nations-Habitat report in which that fact is cited understands what we call suburbs as belonging to an "urban agglomeration" that includes one or more large city centers.[5] The report therefore counts as a city anything from a municipality of 2,000 inhabitants to a "metacity" of more than 20 million. From that point of view, the suburbs that you see are cities. They belong to the same world systems that have produced megacities with vast urban slums.
　　But yes, let's not split hairs. To get back to your question, you are right, there are big differences between what we normally think of as a city and the suburban or exurban towns, villages, and other communities just beyond the trees, shrubbery, grassy berms, and other screening devices that line this highway.

GLAUCON
Wait. I thought that these kinds of U.N. reports only concern themselves with the problems of "developing" countries, not "developed" ones like the United States.

SOCRATES
Again, that distinction is misleading. Everything is related.

GLAUCON

Are you saying, Socrates, that just as there are global cities, there are also global suburbs?

SOCRATES

Yes, but more than that. Every suburb that you see here is global in more than just the economic sense to which we alluded earlier. You may have heard that the 2010 U.S. Census is expected to confirm that what we call America is a dramatic mixture of races, ethnicities, and income groups.[6] Of course, this has been the case for a long time, and cities like New York and Los Angeles have long been global in this sense. But this description now applies very broadly to suburbs as well as to cities. And this mixture are not always melting together like a soup simmering in a big pot. Its various ingredients have in many places remained quite separate. This suburban segregation is spatial, but it is also social, cultural, and economic.

GLAUCON

All right. I recognize that globalization has resulted, in some cases, in more rather than less segregation as communities across the country absorb new immigration. But it has also encouraged a kind of tolerance, where people learn to appreciate, enjoy, and even emulate the values of cultures different from their own.

SOCRATES

Yes, it has. But how far have we come if we have not learned to think outside the categories of "us" and "them"?

GLAUCON

Socrates, you aren't suggesting that we imagine ourselves to be living in one big global village, are you?

SOCRATES

No, far from it. More like the global city you mentioned earlier, where strangers are not feared but welcomed. Or, really, an archipelago of citylike regions connected by transportation and communications infrastructure including highways, rail lines, and fiber-optic networks. Some have called these "megaregions."[7] In addition to the conclusions implied by the U.N. report, another reason to describe these megaregions and the suburbs they contain as cities is that they put the formerly "American" dream in perspective. For example, research shows that many of the inequities that we might normally associate with urban life now apply to suburban life. This is quite noticeable when it comes to housing. Not only have millions of Americans lost their homes to foreclosure, but millions more who now live in the suburbs do not have access to homeownership to begin with, except as a tempting fantasy. And those who choose to rent, or have no choice, are bracketed out of the story. But this dream, with its implied way of living, is only one among many options. And the demographic changes across the suburban landscape remind us that it may be time to dream a different dream.

GLAUCON

Socrates, you are sounding uncharacteristically dogmatic.

SOCRATES

It is only the beginning of a hypothesis. Others who call themselves New Urbanists have already articulated a vision far more comprehensive than my modest suggestion.[8] At its core, however, their vision is predicated on two things: a wistful longing for a bygone era, and homeownership, whether in the economic or the psychological sense. In other words, the American Dream. Though they may deny it, all of their proposals, from the SmartCode to neotraditional design, point in this direction. I am aware that there are dissenters in their ranks who would introduce more "modern" styles into the available architectural vocabulary. But this is secondary, for in the end the cumulative effect of the New Urbanism has been to encourage us to understand our suburbs as villages rather than as cities. Although in principle there may be nothing wrong with this, in practice it allows us to imagine that the suburban subdivisions we pass along the highway do not belong in that U.N. report. In other words, it allows us to imagine that our concerns are merely local ones, rooted in this place and this time, unconnected to what is really going on out there in the world—or indeed at home, as the two are intimately connected.

GLAUCON

Socrates, you have anticipated my argument. But you have not convinced me. I have been reading about these New Urbanists, and they—unlike you—are not dreamers. There is a reason trees have been planted and landscapes maintained to prevent us from seeing the suburban sprawl that stretches along this highway from Maine to Florida: because it's ugly! And the New Urbanists have many sensible suggestions for fixing this; beautifying it, but also making it "smarter," meaning more socially and environmentally responsible. Slightly higher densities, smaller building lots, pedestrian-friendly streets, a lively mixture of activities, greenery: it's not a dream, it's only common sense.

SOCRATES

Glaucon, I did not know you were a New Urbanist!

GLAUCON

Relax. I only attended one of their conferences while

you were holding forth with your drunken friends at the symposium.

SOCRATES
I thought you were there, in Agathon's house.

GLAUCON
No, I left early.

SOCRATES
Okay, well then. Let us return for a moment to our hypothetical suburb. Many architects today like to think of our own hometown, Athens, and its classical environs as a model. But I find the New Urbanist (or neotraditional) idea of a "classical" or Arcadian past to be unrecognizable, whether it refers to ancient Greece or to New England. Have they not read Homer, or Emily Dickinson, or William Carlos Williams for that matter? I realize that I have been harsh on poets in the past, but despite their mimetic tendencies they generally have a better sense of real life in real cities, towns, and villages than anything I have read or seen coming from this Congress for the New Urbanism. That's why you have to watch out for these poets—they are the philosopher's stiffest competition.

Now, had the U.N. existed in classical times, it no doubt would have issued reports confirming that Athens was a sprawling city with a population of about 40,000 citizens. That was not counting women, children, and slaves; its total population may have approached 100,000, which is about the same as that of Athens, Georgia, where we are headed.[9] So even then, Athens was a city, not a town or a village. Yes, it was pedestrian friendly, and something like a democratic debate was possible in its agora and other places of assembly, but only among certain men. It was almost constantly at war with other city-states (as you know, I myself fought in three major battles). And even at home, its citizenry was frequently in upheaval, in which sense it resembled contemporary Athens more than it did a lost classical idyll. Something similar can be said, of course, about the small-town New England of Hawthorne and Dickinson, or the domestic interiors of Poe. These historical cities and towns were places full of conflict, not harmony. Think also of beautiful Savannah, Georgia, just down the road from us. In its heyday, immediately before, during, and after the American Civil War, it was a picturesque town simultaneously riddled with racism and a font of urbane, enlightened culture.[10] No town, city, or country should be forever burdened with the millstone of its past strung around its neck. But many architects, urbanists, politicians, and even real estate developers still seem tempted by the idea of bygone harmonies. And not just the so-called neotraditionalists among them: there is not so much difference between a neoclassical replica of a long-lost past and a modernist replica of one.

But enough of that. You said that the New Urbanist proposals were merely common sense, and of course you are right. But our question should not be "What makes sense under current conditions?" It should be, "How might we change current conditions to make other forms of common sense possible?"

GLAUCON
Socrates, you yourself are not making sense....

SOCRATES
Allow me to explain. As it happens, Athens, Georgia, is the home of the country's first public university, the University of Georgia, where our symposium is being held. It was founded in 1785. Universities—and especially public universities—along with other institutions like a free press are widely considered to be central to the establishment and maintenance of a healthy, democratic public sphere. Now, there are many definitions of the "public sphere." I will use the simplest: the public sphere is the space in which public opinion is formed.[11] Or, if you prefer, it is the space in which common sense is formed, to borrow Thomas Paine's terminology. So you say that many of the ideas now in use to reform American suburbia represent mere common sense. And surely you are right, except that what we take to be common sense is itself constantly being negotiated in the public sphere, or more precisely, in a set of overlapping public spheres. Today's somewhat misleading term for these overlapping spheres is "the media."

It is important to recognize that Enlightenment institutions like universities, the press, even museums, are intimately linked, and that often the knowledge and ideas that circulate as common sense originate in these institutions, only to return there as if from the outside as a challenge to their own dogmas. The credo of architecture, urban design, and urban planning called the New Urbanism is no different: it was largely invented in university lecture halls, museum exhibitions, books, newspaper articles, websites, town hall meetings, civic design competitions, and other sites of public discourse. New Urbanist doctrine now circulates and recirculates through these venues under the guise of common sense.

For example, Glaucon, you and I agree that although suburban sprawl may appear well suited to independent living, it has contributed to many problems in society as a whole. The automobile in which we are driving consumes oil pumped directly out of the earth, in return for which it pumps greenhouse gases directly into the atmosphere. The traffic jam in which we are currently stuck is due in large measure to the fact that nearly everyone here must drive from home to work, or school, or shopping, and back every day, often several times a day. So the design of our environment, with its thousands of houses spread out across thousands of acres of land, contributes directly to this traffic jam. Rivers of asphalt slice through this land, pooling up here and there into vast parking lots, at the center of which float large boxes containing stores, supermarkets, restaurants, offices, schools, hospitals, factories, warehouses, prisons—the elements required for us to live the way we do. Approach the boxes floating in the seas of asphalt on foot and you risk getting run over by a machine operated by a distracted, alienated soul who cannot possibly imagine going home again to the same house in the same cul-de-sac. We have all seen the movie.

And so, yes, it may seem perfectly commonsensical to encourage real estate developers to increase the density of their speculative constructions, and to encourage urban planners to provide streets and spaces that invite, rather than repel, pedestrians. It may even make perfect sense to encourage architects to learn from the past (even if they do choose to ignore history's brutalities) in order to design more comfortable, familiar, and humane environments that reflect a more sane relationship with one another and with the planet. But Glaucon, this is where we disagree. Until we begin to ask why our common sense is so narrow, so limited, indeed so content to settle for so little, we will only postpone the discovery of alternatives, to say nothing about perpetuating the damage.

GLAUCON
What do you mean?

SOCRATES
Consider the public university we are going to visit. Among the many things it represents is the very old idea that education is a public value. Like all public universities in the United States, the University of Georgia is subsidized by taxes. So too was the construction of the highway on which we are driving, as well as the roads leading up to every driveway in the sprawling landscape beyond its landscaped berms. The mortgage on every house at the end of every driveway was, and remains, similarly subsidized through tax-deductible interest that, when seen as what it is intended to be—cash in hand, perhaps to help buy that second car—adds up to one of the largest government grant programs there is.

At some point, people in positions of influence—including politicians and voters but also architects and planners—considered all of this to be common sense. So those who believe that the only options available to us must originate within the marketplace are mistaken. Publicly supported universities, public schools, even the interstate highway system all hint at other options. But these options will only become viable if values other than financial profit become common sense, and that can only happen in and through a reclaimed public sphere.

> GLAUCON
> That sounds radical.

> SOCRATES
> No, not really. Phrased another way, is it not very modest to expect that a full range of options available for designing and planning our suburbs and cities be placed on the table for public discussion? In fact, is that not just common sense?

From House to Housing

INT. CAR INTERSTATE 95 — LATER STILL THAT AFTERNOON
Socrates and Glaucon are still stuck in traffic. There is shouting on the radio.

> GLAUCON
> Well. All I know is, my home is my castle.

> SOCRATES
> You're not really going to go there, are you?

> GLAUCON
> Yes. I do mean it.

> SOCRATES
> What do you mean by it?

> GLAUCON
> That beyond the simple, commonsense idea that people should live in houses, the single-family house is a kind of symbol—a monument to a way of life.

> SOCRATES
> So it is.

> GLAUCON
> And although it could be planned better, designed better, built better, the house is all we've got, in the end.

SOCRATES
By "we," do you mean the general public?

GLAUCON
No, I mean each of us, as individuals.

SOCRATES
What about the car?

GLAUCON
It's a kind of appendage of the house.

SOCRATES
And the home entertainment center?

GLAUCON
The same. Cars, computers, television sets: all of these life-style amenities are designed to plug into the house—most of them literally. But not only does the house contain all these personal belongings, it represents the life savings of many families, acquired through hard work and thrift. It's like an appendage of the self. Which brings us back to the question of ownership. You know, you nearly convinced me that the house is not a special kind of commodity and deserving of the special kind of protection it's received. But seen in *this* context....

SOCRATES
Let me ask you, is the house an appendage of yourself if you rent it, or share it in some other way? Or only if you own it?

GLAUCON
Both. Because the symbolic equation between "house" and "home" is reinforced by that psychological sense of ownership you spoke about earlier. We might even say that this psychological sense of ownership is more important than actual economic ownership when it comes to houses. That, after all, is what the bank is selling you when it grants you a mortgage—the right to say that you "own" your home, when in fact you do not.

SOCRATES
Yes, Glaucon, that is correct. You have helped prove my point: that what we feel about houses and homes is as important as what we think about them. That, again, explains the rivalry between poets and philosophers.

GLAUCON
But that is also why the single-family house is fundamental to the way we live. It represents the ideal of psychological ownership around which our suburbs, and our financial system, are built. What we need are better houses, which will lead to better, smarter suburbs. In other words, what today's house needs is a better architect.

SOCRATES

An architect who learns from past examples and past mistakes.

GLAUCON

Correct.

SOCRATES

And who would that architect be?

GLAUCON

I do not know. But I do know that such an architect would first and foremost be able to express the fundamental equation between house and home.

SOCRATES

That equation is not fundamental. It is conventional. Though it may seem a matter of common sense, we have already shown it to be subject to change through public discussion and debate, so long as every actual option is on the table.

GLAUCON

No. What I mean is that the equation between house and home, especially when beautifully rendered by a skilled architect, corresponds with a fundamental metaphysical truth that we experience as a psychological sense of homeownership. We therefore take greater care of the place where we live, and we look out for the safety of our neighbors and of others around us, which also ensures, by the way, that property values in the neighborhood remain stable, thus protecting our investment.

SOCRATES

Yes. Common sense. But let us return again to our hypothetical suburb. Imagine for a moment that the houses lining its byways are described as what they are: housing. In other words, though they may afford their inhabitants a sense of belonging, even a sense of what you call "home," they are, like the streets on which we drive, ultimately part of the infrastructure of the city or suburb. This does not mean that the houses are publicly owned, though they could be, since in any case many of them are now actually owned by publicly supported financial institutions. It means that, like other infrastructures (including roads, rail lines, and fiber-optic cables, but also hospitals, schools, and parks), they belong to the public realm, regardless of who actually owns them.

By this I do not only mean that you can see the houses from the street. That would imply that all we need to do is add a porch to address the alienation of suburban life. I mean that just as we found something global inside the single-family suburban house, we find something public inside it as well. Here I mainly have in mind an extension of the idea of the public sphere we were discussing earlier. For what actually happens inside houses? Among other things, people talk on the phone, read newspapers, watch television, listen to the radio, surf the Internet, check email, text-message, tweet, and so on.

Now of course these things don't only happen inside houses, but houses and apartments are a major site for the exchange of ideas and information in this way. Occasionally these house-dwellers might even sit around a table and have a traditional conversation among themselves, or with their invited guests. When they discuss ideas, including ideas about possible houses and possible cities, they are essentially doing what you and I are doing right now, inside our car. They are engaging in public conversation, however privately. That is, they are imagining that others, perhaps sitting at another table in another house reading the same newspaper or watching the same program, share their ideas. They are, in short, imagining themselves as part of a larger community with shared feelings, shared ideas, and shared interests. An older name for such a community would have been a "nation." Hence the concept of the American Dream, which is actually dreamed in public, around tables, on couches, in front of screens, and in houses. And the type of community dreamed in these spaces can—and does—change every day.

GLAUCON
So you are saying that what makes the house public, and hence negotiable as a concept, is the very same dream of ownership, whether real or psychological, that I argued made it private and hence unassailable?

SOCRATES
Yes.

GLAUCON
Socrates, you are going in circles.

SOCRATES
No, I am merely stating the obvious—that what you call a house is merely one form of housing among many, with no special symbolic, social, or economic status. This is different from saying that it is merely one commodity among many, since its public character also affords it a type of value that is exempt from market determinations.

GLAUCON
All right, but nearly all of the elements that make up your "public sphere" are brought to us by the markets. Newspapers, television, wireless communication, the Internet: these are all privately owned infrastructures, not public ones.

SOCRATES

Yes, they are. But like houses themselves, they all possess a public character that is not entirely measured by their price, their profit, or their owner. Only the house—the space where it all occurs—seems to be largely exempt from this. It is, as you say, your castle. But we have already seen that your psychological sense of ownership was only made possible by a heavy government subsidy in the first place.

GLAUCON

Not mine. I earned every penny, and I don't need any help from the government, thank you very much.

SOCRATES

We'll see about that. But first, we must finish with our house. Let us consider its architecture more closely. Not its style, but its logic. Where, for example, do you suppose the front door is?

GLAUCON

I am tempted to offer a commonsense answer: on the front, of course. But I suspect there's a trick.

SOCRATES

You are learning, Glaucon. You have begun to understand that there is little that is commonsensical about today's houses. Indeed, the front door to many of them is located not on the front (this is merely an auxiliary or ceremonial entrance) but on the side, next to the driveway, or even inside the garage. This reflects the actual intimacy between car and house. What is our architect to do about this? Tradition stipulates that the front door be located on the front, preferably behind a gracious porch. But everyday life, centered on the automobile, dictates otherwise. Does our architect recognize this and convert the garage entrance into a monumental architectural event? Or do we redesign our entire city and with it, our entire way of life, so that the car vanishes and the front door regains its place of honor on the front again?

GLAUCON

The latter, I suspect.

SOCRATES

But beware. This is a false choice, a rhetorical device that might suit our Sophistic friends. The fact that we can even imagine restoring a nonexistent idyll built around the front porch by thoroughly transforming our transportation systems suggests that there are many more options available to us; some more dramatic, some less. My point is that every detail of every house is in some way connected to a larger system. That is what makes every house a form of housing, a piece of infrastructure linked up to other infrastructures from the driveway or the living room.

GLAUCON
Yes, but for modern architects, "housing" usually connotes mass housing—large apartment blocks, often built for workers, or for the poor. In America this is still called public housing, even though much of it has been privatized.

SOCRATES
These housing blocks, or "projects" as they are sometimes also called, are only one type among many possible types of housing that do not necessarily need to be isolated in the city. One of the core assumptions of architectural modernism was that in the name of rational planning, activities such as work, living, and recreation should be separated from one another into urban zones. We now know that this type of separation is not necessarily rational, just as we also know, from our reflection on the house, that many diverse activities take place there every day. In the suburbs, this irrational form of rationalized separation contributed to sprawl. When we understand that the house is a basic unit of suburban development through which people, goods, and energy all circulate, we begin to grasp how these types of cities might be redesigned.

functional separation

Change the Dream and You Change the City

INT. CAR INTERSTATE 95 — LATER STILL THAT AFTERNOON
Socrates and Glaucon are still stuck in traffic. The talk on the radio turns to Wall Street.

GLAUCON
This idea of the house—or, as you call it, housing—as the basic unit of urbanization leads me to think that architects and urbanists ought to devote their considerable energies and talents to perfecting this building type. Can we not design a "smarter" house today, when we have so many more resources and technologies at our disposal than we did in ancient Athens, or in old New

41   The Buell Hypothesis

England, or even in antebellum Santa Fe for that matter? Humans have changed little since these earlier times, and so it remains our task to deduce the essence of human habitation as it might be contained in a house, and thence to build a new type of city out of this new type of house.

SOCRATES
Not exactly, my friend, for this returns us to where we began, with our reflections on the idea of "home" as it relates to the larger world. Although there are dwellings nearly everywhere on earth, and although the humans occupying these dwellings possess many similar characteristics, there is also much that differentiates them, inside and out. As you know, the associated philosophical problem is classically posed as one of the universal versus the particular. But it is not as simple as saying that all people (meaning all races, classes, genders, cultures, and other social groups) are essentially the same or essentially different. As we have already seen inside our hypothetical suburban house, even the simplest idea of "home" that we might think unifies all people is fraught with internal tensions and conflicts. So, too, with any "hometown" or "homeland." This does not mean that any and all forms of unity simply break apart upon closer inspection. The situation is more paradoxical than that. The conflicts themselves form a type of social bond, if they are allowed to play themselves out in reasonable ways, through dialogue and the exchange of views rather than through force.

GLAUCON
That sounds even more utopian than my notion of an ideal home.

SOCRATES
And so it may be. But it is also more realistic, since that is what actually happens in houses and cities all over the world. As everyone knows, the living room is a contested space. As is the shopping mall parking lot. As is the air we breathe, with its pollutants and its greenhouse gases. The ability to recognize difference and yet engage in a dialogue over conflicts large and small is a mark of maturity, not of idleness.

Although all of this may seem more a matter for political philosophers or sociologists than for architects, you have correctly identified the central role that architecture can play here as an art form rather than as a form of social engineering. Recall that even you conceded that a psychological sense of ownership was as important as actual ownership when it came down to establishing a sense of "home." From this we concluded that how we feel about houses is as important as what we do with them. I am merely suggesting that we learn to feel differently about our houses, on the basis of the

architecture
art / social engineering

42

observation that there is little that is ultimately timeless about how we feel about them or how we use them in the first place. Like poetry, architecture helps us to understand and elaborate these feelings, and hence to experiment with them and to change them. This is why, like poetry, architecture can challenge any well-established social and political order, including that which reigns in a suburban cul-de-sac.

So rather than expelling the architects along with the poets from our hypothetical suburb, we ought to invite them back in to participate in our expanded public sphere. We have already concluded that this suburb is anything but ideal, though it is no doubt home to many thousands of people, all of whom have formed some kind of attachment to it regardless of how they feel about traffic jams and parking lots. These feelings are genuine and ought to be respected. But they also ought to be examined, since, as we have already observed, suburbs are increasingly home to many millions across the country who are not the immediate beneficiaries of the emotionally charged American Dream to which the policies that created these places were dedicated. We might even consider these millions of people its victims, to the extent that this dream is offered as the only alternative, even though it is hardly within reach of everyone.

GLAUCON
What are you suggesting, then? That we assemble everyone together in a town hall and air our differences on housing policy, property, and urbanization in a civil tone?

SOCRATES
That seems unlikely, since (with the exception of the contribution made by the New Urbanists) such a debate is largely nonexistent. We have to start from the beginning. When was the last time you heard the term "public housing" used in a positive way on television? And yet it would be reasonable to expect that option, or something very close to it, to be up for discussion in the wake of a mortgage-foreclosure crisis. But public housing has accumulated such a stigma—some of which is justified, some of which is not—that it is nearly impossible even to contemplate it publicly without eliciting a heated response. Imagine, public housing in the suburbs! The thought of it! But such housing already exists, in its classic form as well as in the form of federally subsidized single-family houses. Why should some new, equitable form of public housing not be more widely available as an option for those who cannot afford homeownership?

There is no reason to be defensive about this, nor to apologize for the residual but popular traces of the welfare state in the same breath as one apologizes for its supposed failures in the area of housing. Again, it is not simply a question of the role of government

public housing

versus that of the market. It is a question of what sort of thoughts we allow ourselves to think, publicly and privately. Your colleagues at the Congress for the New Urbanism understood this when they repackaged the American Dream. It is why their most important triumph was the major change in federal public housing policy that resulted in the ironically titled Homeownership Opportunities for People Everywhere (or HOPE VI) legislation.

Essentially, HOPE VI replaced the image of the public housing "projects" with images of "home" as a matter of law.[12] In doing so, it acknowledged a basic truth, that what we call "home" is always defined in opposition to something else, which in this case was represented by the "projects." (I can hear something similar in your desire to distinguish "house" from "housing," psychologically as well as typologically.) By superimposing the imagery and format of the single-family house on public housing, the HOPE VI legislation seeks to repress the social and economic conflicts that remain hidden within the opposition of "house" (as "home") versus "housing" (as an institution). During most of the twentieth century, these were expressed as the tension between living independently versus living collectively. But the imagery ingrained in our minds, of massive public housing projects being spectacularly demolished as failed social experiments, is also the imagery of somebody's home being demolished. Imagine, if you will, that the foreclosure crisis led to the demolition of every house in a distressed suburban subdivision: the American suburb as a failed social experiment. Even if they understood its many problems, how do you think its inhabitants would feel?

The theatrical demolition of public housing projects, which is financed by the well-meaning HOPE VI legislation, is symbolically charged. The partial replacement of these projects with mixed-income, neotraditional neighborhoods, which is dictated by the legislation, must therefore be seen as a form of aesthetic therapy. This is one reason why its architecture matters.

GLAUCON
Socrates, I have never heard you speak so psychologically about art.

SOCRATES
That is only the tip of the iceberg. Deeper down are the thoughts and feelings that are expressed when we say offhandedly that a particular house or city is beautiful. Historically, suburbs partly originated with such feelings, which were evoked by design in highly technical ways. For when we speak of architecture and urbanism, from the design of buildings to the design of urban policy, we are always speaking about a volatile mixture of art

destruction of housing

and technology. This mixture has social consequences partly because social life itself is built around many such mixtures. The American Dream is one of their effects. It acquires its meaning largely through the mystique of the ideal home, which is both artistic and technological in character.

So there is great opportunity for architects and urbanists, working together with other intellectuals and professionals as well as with housing residents, activists, and citizens, to transform the landscapes we have been discussing. These landscapes exist in the mind as much as they do on the ground, not merely as private fantasies but as public ones. Architecture is central to this process. That is why, stuck in traffic with time on our hands, I have found it amusing to develop, step by step, a hypothesis that puts the architecture of housing at the center of a public debate.

GLAUCON
Could you summarize the hypothesis, please?

SOCRATES
Certainly. First, the fact that we live in a globalized age not only means that big changes are taking place in the world out there, it also means that things are changing in here, at home. We have experienced some of these changes directly, through the realizations that individual homeownership is closely linked to international finance and that the mixtures of people living in suburban neighborhoods are changing.

Hence, what we typically call a suburb is actually a type of city, not only because it is recorded as such in official reports but also because it possesses attributes that we normally associate with urban life. Along with demographic and economic diversity, these include contestation over values and overlapping spheres of interest and activity. Somewhat surprisingly, these overlaps occur inside as well as outside the house (as our parable of the elusive front door suggests). What we call the public sphere—or the space in which public opinion is formed—penetrates deep into every living room and kitchen. In this sense, the dining room table is among the most public of places to discuss the future of houses and cities. So, too, the front seat of a car.

That the house is actually a type of housing and that housing is a form of infrastructure both follow from this—first, in the sense that the private house, like the public "dream" to which it corresponds, is just as institutionalized within social and economic policy as is a public housing complex; and second, in the sense that the same house is tightly plugged into far-reaching economic, social, and technological systems without which it would not exist. Reciprocally, these systems rely on the house and its corresponding dream for their own existence.

The Hypothesis

home ownership

international finance

suburb is city

front seat of car

house = public housing infrastructure

45   The Buell Hypothesis

change the dream

Hence, change the dream and you change the city. Architecture offers a highly effective medium through which to contemplate possible futures in this regard. There are many ways in which we can imagine housing differently, from the way it is financed to the way it is designed to the way it is combined with or separated from other spaces in which other activities occur. Many of these possibilities imply systemic change at the urban, regional, national, or international levels. But that is for later.

For now, it looks like the traffic is starting to move, Glaucon, so we had better look out for our exit. I will call Diotima and tell her that we are running late. They can start the symposium without us.

FADE OUT

1. This was one of the many criticisms of modern architecture made by advocates of postmodernism, most often by implication. See, for example, Charles Jencks's often cited discussion of the demolition of the Pruitt-Igoe housing complex, St. Louis, in 1972, in *The Language of Post-Modern Architecture* (London: Academy Editions, 1977), p. 9.

2. The most relevant text is Plato's *Republic,* trans. G. M. A. Grube, rev. C. D. C. Reeve (Indianapolis: Hackett, 1992). See also Plato's *Symposium,* trans. Alexander Nehamas and Paul Woodruff (Indianapolis: Hackett, 1989). This dialogue loosely adapts aspects of the Socratic model; it does not fully reproduce its format or style. The characters are likewise loose adaptations.

3. Federal lands constitute about 34 percent of the total land area of the United States and about 27 percent of the land area in the continental United States. Data on federally owned land is available at: National Atlas of the United States, "Raw Data Download," United States Department of the Interior, http://www.nationalatlas.gov/atlasftp.html.

4. Among the many studies of suburbanization in the United States, see in particular Robert A. Beauregard, *When American Became Suburban* (Minneapolis: University of Minnesota Press, 2006); Dolores Hayden, *A Field Guide to Sprawl* (New York: W.W. Norton, 2004); Robert Fishman, *Bourgeois Utopias: The Rise and Fall of Suburbia* (New York: Basic Books, 1989); and Kenneth T. Jackson, *Crabgrass Frontier: The Suburbanization of the United States* (New York: Oxford University Press, 1987). See also Ellen Dunham-Jones and June Williamson, *Retrofitting Suburbia: Urban Design Solutions for Redesigning Suburbs* (New York: John Wiley & Sons, 2009).

5. United Nations Human Settlements Programme (UN-HABITAT), *The State of the World's Cities Report 2006/2007: 30 Years of Shaping the Habitat Agenda* (London and Sterling, Va.: Earthscan, 2006). See also United Nations Human Settlements Programme (UN-HABITAT), *State of the World's Cities 2008/2009: Harmonious Cities* (London and Sterling, Va.: Earthscan, 2008).

6. Findings for the 2010 U.S. Census are available on the Census Bureau's website, at http://factfinder2.census.gov/main.html.

7. Richard Florida, Tim Gulden, and Charlotta Mellander, "The Rise of the Mega Region," unpublished paper, The Martin Prosperity Institute, Joseph L. Rotman School of Management, University of Toronto, October 2007. Available online at http://www.rotman.utoronto.ca/userfiles/prosperity/File/Rise.of.%20the.Mega-Regions.w.cover.pdf.

8. There is a substantial literature outlining the principles of the New Urbanism. Among the most relevant works is Andres Duany, Elizabeth Plater-Zyberk, and Jeff Speck, *Suburban Nation: The Rise of Sprawl and the Decline of the American Dream*, 2nd ed. (New York: North Point Press, 2010). See also: Congress for the New Urbanism, *The Charter of the New Urbanism* (New York: McGraw Hill, 1999); Peter Calthorpe, *The Next American Metropolis: Ecology, Community, and the American Dream* (New York: Princeton Architectural Press, 1993); and Peter Katz, *The New Urbanism* (New York: McGraw Hill, 1993).

9. The principal study on the population of classical Athens remains A. W. Gomme, *The Population of Athens in the Fifth and Fourth Centuries B.C.*, 1933 (reprint ed. Chicago: Argonaut, 1967). Gomme estimates the combined population of Athens and Piraeus to have ranged between 155,000 and 168,000 between 430 and 330 B.C.E. This would include between 50,000 and 60,000 citizens. However, more recent scholarship suggests that around 430 B.C.E. these numbers could have been considerably lower, between 35,000 and 40,000 citizens in Athens and about 25,000 in Piraeus. See Ian Morris, "The Growth of Greek Cities in the First Millennium B.C.," Princeton/Stanford Working Papers in Classics, December 2005. Available at http://www.princeton.edu/~pswpc/pdfs/morris/120509.pdf. In 2006 the United States Census Bureau estimated the population of consolidated Athens-Clarke County, Georgia, at 111,580. See http://quickfacts.census.gov/qfd/states/13/1303440.html.

10. See, for example, Walter J. Fraser Jr., *Savannah in the Old South* (Athens: University of Georgia Press, 2003). Symptomatically, the author believes that "mitigating the violence and brutality that sometimes flashed like summer lightning across Savannah were the city's private and public structures and spaces, which acted as humanizing influences." See p. 343.

11. The classic definition of the public sphere as "the realm of our social life in which something approaching public opinion can be formed" is to be found in Jürgen Habermas, "The Public Sphere: An Encyclopedia Article," 1964, trans. Sare Lennox and Frank Lennox, *New German Critique 3* (Autumn 1974):49. See also Habermas, *The Structural Transformation of the Public Sphere: An Inquiry into a Category of Bourgeois Society*, trans. Thomas Burger with Frederick Lawrence (Cambridge, Mass.: The MIT Press, 1989). More recently, Bruno Latour has built on a related American tradition, stemming from debates between Walter Lippmann and John Dewey, to describe networks of actors and artifacts assembled into a body politic through public debate. See especially Latour and Peter Weibel, eds., *Making Things Public: Atmospheres of Democracy* (Cambridge, Mass.: The MIT Press, 2005).

12. For an overview of the history and scope of American housing policy, including the HOPE VI program, see Alex F. Schwartz, *Housing Policy in the United States*, 2nd ed. (New York: Routledge, 2010).

In late 2008, the United States Congress and the Federal Reserve responded dramatically to the growing financial crisis. The Troubled Asset Relief Program (TARP) legislation that bailed out many of the country's banks did so because, as the value of individual properties sank, so did bank assets represented by bundled subprime, alternative-A, and other high-interest mortgages. It was largely the state of the country's housing, and housing markets, that led many to wonder whether these banks were, indeed, too big to be allowed to fail. After the bailout came economic stimulus. The maps in this section situate the *Foreclosed* workshop in this context, at the national scale. They reflect conditions on the day the federal stimulus was signed, partly to indicate roads not taken since that time.

A residential foreclosure crisis followed from the initial subprime mortgage crisis. In 2008, there were over 3 million foreclosure filings on homes (fig. 1), an increase of 81 percent over 2007 and 225 percent over 2006, when subprime mortgages peaked and then started their rapid decline.[1] On February 17, 2009, President Barack Obama signed the American Recovery and Reinvestment Act (ARRA) followed the next day by the Making Home Affordable Act (MHA). Where MHA sought to stem foreclosure with provisions for mortgage restructuring and refinancing, ARRA hoped to stimulate the economy by investing in new infrastructures, creating jobs with that stimulus, and preparing the economy in the long run with funding for more environmentally sustainable technologies. Yet housing was surprisingly absent from the stimulus legislation, with the exception of a relatively small investment in updating existing public housing, mostly to ensure better environmental performance. The government's role in this area remained limited largely to minimizing the damage incurred under market conditions, rather than direct intervention.

Fig. 1

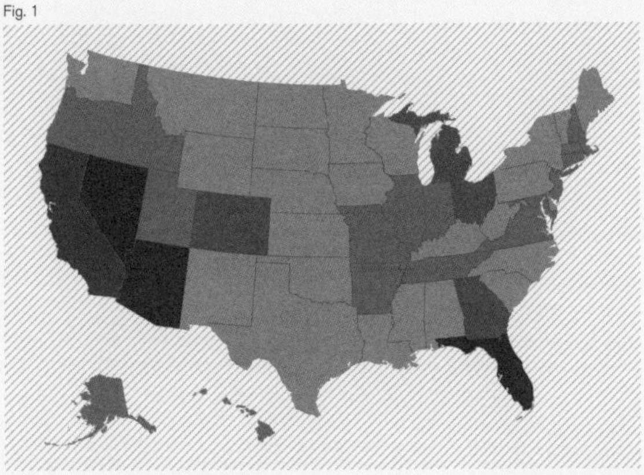

2008 foreclosure rate by state

0   1   2   3   4%

[handwritten annotation: housing absent from stimulus]

Fig. 2

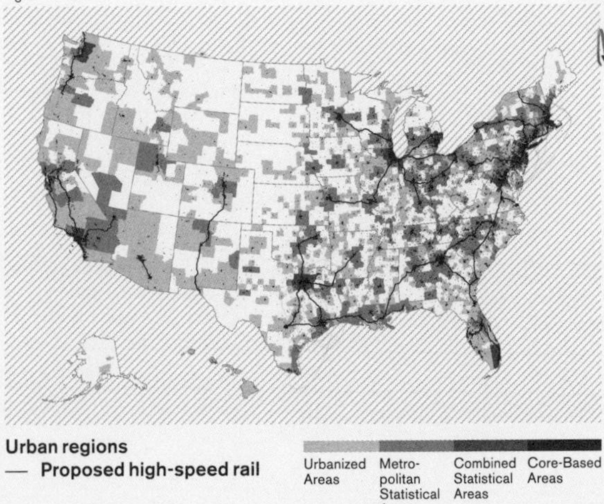

Urban regions
— Proposed high-speed rail

Urbanized Areas | Metropolitan Statistical Areas | Combined Statistical Areas | Core-Based Areas

Megaregions

The existing and proposed high-speed rail lines supported by ARRA would connect the country's megaregions, which are made up of multiple cities and their suburbs grouped within an area (fig. 2).[2] These regions increasingly function economically and culturally as units, regardless of how they may intersect state lines. No longer does a town's local economy simply reflect the revenue generated within its own boundaries; today that economy benefits both its state and its region.

Each of the eight suburban municipalities documented in the original *Buell Hypothesis*, of which five

Fig. 3

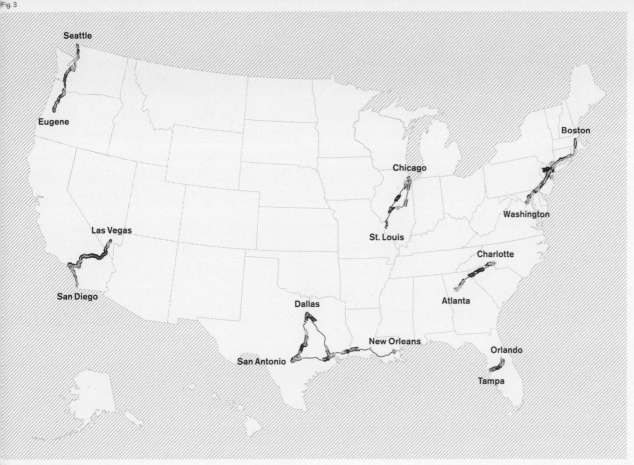

Case study corridors
— Proposed high-speed rail
▓ Multi-criteria decision analysis results

were studied in the *Foreclosed* workshop, is located within one of these megaregions. The municipalities are: Rialto, California; Tomball, Texas; Chamblee and Doraville, Georgia; Temple Terrace, Florida; Landover, Maryland; the Oranges, New Jersey; Cicero, Illinois; and Keizer, Oregon. Ultimately, Rialto, Temple Terrace, the Oranges, Cicero, and Keizer were selected as sites by workshop participants. All of these municipalities are situated along an existing or proposed rail line connecting the large urban centers that act as regional anchors.

Crisis: Multi-Criteria Decision Analysis
Each suburb represents a particular aspect of the more general crisis, where high foreclosure rates are only one indicator of systemic housing need, imbalance, or inequity. Each also offers potential for long-term investment and growth, and hence an opportunity to redefine the problem and to propose new solutions. Taken together, these suburbs should therefore be seen as representative of the overall situation, but each in a somewhat different way. In order to distinguish what is typical in each case from what is unique, they were chosen through Multi-Criteria Decision Analysis (MCDA),

a method that combines an array of quantitative and qualitative factors (fig. 3).

The analysis was based on information collected from the 2000 U.S. Census and the 2008 American Community Survey.[3] Though the results of the 2010 Census were unavailable at the time of the original research, they largely confirm the long-term trends indicated by the initial findings. The MCDA combines social, economic, and housing demographics. These include population and population density, the prevalence of detached single-family homes, local vacancy rates, local renting rates, average household size and the percentage of those households that are occupied by families, the percentage of the population that is either elderly or children, median household income and poverty rates, households receiving public assistance and supplemental security income, commute times to work and the means of transportation used for those commutes, the prevalence of new residents (who moved into the area within the last year) and from how far away they moved, race, ethnicity, and educational attainment. The analysis also factors in the mortgage status for owner-occupied homes, meaning how many mortgages homeowners

49   The Buell Hypothesis

Fig. 4

Keizer, Oregon
▒ MCDA results
— State boundaries

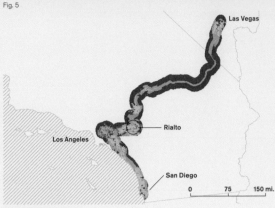

Fig. 5

Rialto, California
▒ MCDA results
— State boundaries

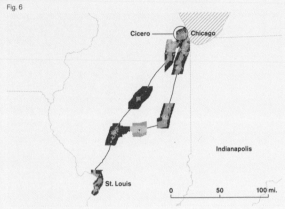

Fig. 6

Cicero, Illinois
▒ MCDA results
— State boundaries

Fig. 7

Temple Terrace, Florida
▒ MCDA results
— State boundaries

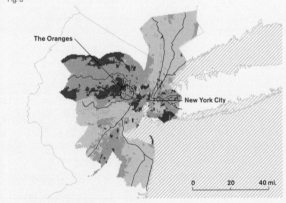

Fig. 8

The Oranges, New Jersey
▒ MCDA results
— State boundaries

carried and whether they also had home equity loans. This last criterion offers a way of understanding how many homeowners used their homes as an investment, or as collateral for further borrowing. For each of the variables, available data as of February 2009 was compared with information from 2000 to isolate the areas that showed both current need for investment and significant recent change calling for more investment.[4]

In the resulting maps, the "hot spots" shown in red denote areas of particular interest. This narrowed down the search for representative case studies from several thousand to only a handful per megaregion and allowed for qualitative comparisons among those remaining. During this qualitative phase, each suburb with a high score was examined for its local history, economic base, and development patterns, as well as for how it was weathering the foreclosure and financial crisis.

In the end, one representative suburb was chosen per region. Each would benefit from a new high-speed rail corridor passing within its boundaries. Each would also benefit greatly from a significant investment in housing and other forms of urban infrastructure to

Fig. 9

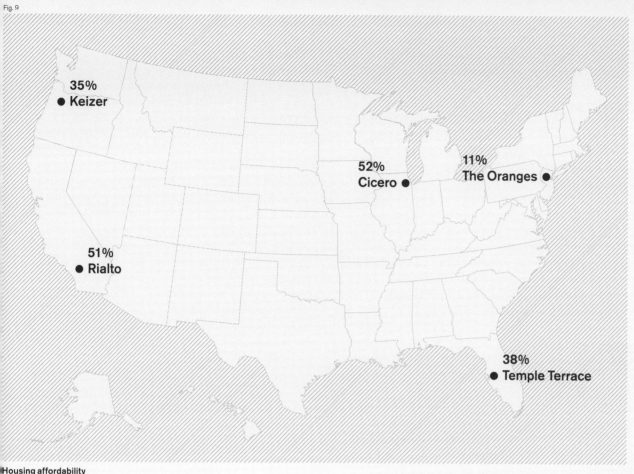

Housing affordability
●   Case study suburbs
%   Households that cannot afford monthly housing costs

complement the potential investment in regional transportation. The five municipalities that actually became
sites for the workshop participants are highlighted here
(figs. 4–8).

Housing Affordability
Finally, the initial research showed what "housing affordability" means in these locales. The common definition of
"affordability" requires that a household spend no more
than thirty percent of its monthly income on housing.[5]
Fig. 9 shows the percentage of households in each of the
study's municipalities that could not afford its housing
costs as of February 2009. While homeowners everywhere are today having a more difficult time affording
their mortgages, in each of the case studies it is actually
the renting households that spend the greatest percentage of their income on the roof over their heads. This not
only indicates an affordability gap for homeowners, it
draws an increasingly uncrossable line between those
who have the means to access what, in another, less
technical parlance, is commonly called the American
Dream and those who do not.

Local vs. National vs. Global
These facts reflect systemic issues at all scales, from
the local to the global, mediated by federal, state, and
municipal legislation, employment and immigration
patterns, international finance markets, and many other
factors. But also lurking behind these figures are cultural
values that often go unquestioned. That is why we have
attempted to portray, through these case studies, the
general crisis in its specific manifestations.

Each of the case studies offers a different angle on
this crisis. Together they stretch across the entire conti-
nent, from California to Illinois to Florida. To some extent
each reflects the peculiarities of its region in terms of climate, economy, politics, and so on. Each also possesses
a different history. Some areas have grown dramatically
in the recent past. Others anticipate significant future
growth. Still others are older suburbs that have under-
gone notable demographic transformation in recent
years. So there is nothing especially typical about any of
these. In fact, it is clear from such evidence that there is
no such thing as a "typical" American suburb.[6]

And yet many processes bind these and other such
places together into larger urban systems. To begin with,

<30%
Dream

51   The Buell Hypothesis

there are the roads, airports, rail lines, and other infrastructures that connect towns and cities and allow us to see each as part of a sprawling megaregion, and evidence of a much larger pattern that has emerged in the midst of the suburban sprawl.

In each of these cases we also see variations on the theme of homeownership and imagined independence, along with evidence of conflict and dispossession. Contrary to the stereotype that only inner cities or remote rural areas are plagued with economic or social distress, each of these suburban areas struggles with relatively high poverty rates, compounded by high foreclosure rates. Some are also quite segregated, with more affluent neighborhoods on one side of the proverbial "tracks" and less affluent neighborhoods on the other. Often, such segmentations are crisscrossed with the subliminal tensions as well as the innovations of multiracial, multiethnic suburban life. They also reflect persistent patterns of gender inequity that remain typical, rather than exceptional, in housing distribution and access throughout the country. This despite decades of work in these areas, probably because most of that work has drawn its models from urban examples.[7]

Layers

There is not a unified pattern of home foreclosures in these suburbs, although each exhibits relatively high rates when compared to the national average. This suggests that though its effects are most immediately felt, home foreclosure sits on the irregular tip of a much larger iceberg. We can call this iceberg the "housing system," a term that encompasses every form of dwelling from individual homes to large apartment complexes, privately or publicly owned. This system is clearly linked with the other systems that configure cities. These can be entered at any point, from which all of the other systems can be accessed. Look at a single house and you'll see not only the city of which it is a part but an entire economy and an entire set of social structures in which its inhabitants participate. So rather than a single, monolithic "iceberg," it may be better to imagine a set of overlapping landscapes, in which the uneven terrain of home foreclosure intersects with the uneven terrain of economic opportunity and with the uneven terrain of cultural values, like a pastry whose layers pass through one another, up and down in irregular undulations.

It is difficult to see patterns in such undulations. Yet the Buell research shows that the physical, social, and economic particularities of each of these places all have a role to play in situating that place in the larger field of forces called suburbia. In each, the forces have converged in different ways to paint a portrait of a crisis reverberating through that field. Given the interpenetration of layers, what can be understood as a housing crisis, part of a larger economic crisis, also appears as a cultural crisis, or a conflict between different dreams.

Changing the Frame

This is how we can reflect, by implication, on the much discussed American Dream through the hard, persistent facts of suburban reality. In these facts, we discern the outlines of a debate that has not yet occurred. A look at the master plans developed by many of these municipalities, with their "win-win" visions of mass-marketed bucolic bliss, begs the question: What is wrong with this picture? Possibly, what is wrong is not so much the picture but the frame, or the default into the story that the urban future is one in which markets rule, states defer, and NGOs look after the damage. This brief summary therefore records, on the ground, the persistence of that very simple, effective plot line. Such stories have real effects, not the least of which involves placing very real limits on the imaginations of architects, economists, politicians, and citizens alike.

1. See Stephanie Armour, "2008 Foreclosure Filings Set Record," USA Today, February 3, 2009. Online at http://www.usatoday.com/money/economy/ housing/2009-01-14-foreclosure-record-filings_N.htm.

2. See Richard Florida, Tim Gulden, and Charlotta Mellander, "The Rise of the Mega Region," unpublished paper, The Martin Prosperity Institute, Joseph L. Rotman School of Management, University of Toronto, October 2007. Available online at http://www.rotman.utoronto.ca/userfiles/prosperity/File/Rise.of .%20the.Mega-Regions.w.cover.pdf.

3. Data sets from the 2000 U.S. Decennial Census Summary File 3 and 2008 American Community Survey 1-Year Estimates were downloaded for the listed variables from the U.S. Census website's download center. For the 2000 data sets, information was downloaded by census block group, with the exception of the Northeast Corridor analysis, which, owing to the size of the study area, utilized county subdivisions. For the 2008 data sets, information was downloaded by counties. To enable comparative analysis, data from the 2000 census block groups was aggregated by county. The U.S. Census Bureau's Download Center can be found online at http://factfinder.census.gov/servlet/DownloadDatasetServlet ?_lang=en.

4. Once individual study areas were identified through the multi-criteria decision analysis, additional foreclosure data sets were purchased by zip code from RealtyTrac within the date range of February 1–28, 2009. These included properties transferred to lender ownership during the month of February 2009 within the zip codes enclosed by or intersecting each municipality's boundaries.

5. See U.S. Department of Housing and Urban Development Office of Community Planning and Development, "Affordable Housing," U.S. Department of Housing and Urban Development, online at http://www.hud.gov/offices/cpd/ affordablehousing/.

6. See p. 46, note 4, for literature on the historical texture of suburbanization in the United States.

7. On gender and suburbanization, see Gwendolyn Wright, Building the Dream: A Social History of Housing in America (Cambridge: MIT Press, 1981), and Dolores Hayden, Redesigning the American Dream: The Future of Housing, Work, and Family Life, 2nd ed. (New York: W. W. Norton & Co., 2002).

PROJECTS

markets rule
statis defer.
NGO's repair the damage

THE ORANGES N.J.

Thoughts on a Walking City project

- - - - The Oranges municipal boundaries
Publicly supported development sites

The greater New York City region is in many ways anomalous in relation to the rest of the country, but its sheer size, in both area and population, makes it important in investigations of suburban and metropolitan growth and life-styles. While other studies here addressed regions with developing transportation networks, it also made sense to include one in which an extensive commuter rail system is already in place. More specifically, as the United States consolidates into regions that cross state boundaries, the New York–New Jersey relationship offers an important precedent in suburban commuting as developed over time. This was the only case study conducted on existing commuter lines. Northeast Corridor express trains already stop in New York, and existing, local mass transit makes that rail line accessible to neighborhoods in New Jersey.

The analysis led to the four Oranges for qualitative as well as quantitative reasons. Orange (also called the City of Orange), South Orange, East Orange, and West Orange share a history but diverge in their identities.[1] They are small municipalities that are demographically distinct but closely identified with one another. The Oranges share access to the same rail line, which may inform development strategies within their boundaries. At the same time, these municipalities are long-established suburbs of a nearby city, or actually two cities—New York and nearby Newark.

Local Economy

The local economies of the Oranges vary from east to west. Generally speaking, South and West Orange are the more affluent of the four, with household median incomes more than double those of Orange and East Orange. While it is difficult to summarize the economic variations among the four municipalities, the primary industries in each are education, health care, and social assistance, which range from 24 to 27 percent of jobs. In early 2009, unemployment in the Oranges ranged from roughly 6 percent in South Orange and West Orange to 10 percent in Orange to almost 16 percent in East Orange. These economic differences, as well as variations in housing density, surely help to explain the heavy foreclosure pattern in East Orange, and to the east and north of it in parts of Newark (fig. 1).

Local Conditions

The poverty rates in Orange and East Orange resemble those of neighboring Newark more closely than those of the other Oranges, with a pocket of increased poverty near one possible development site in South Orange (fig. 2). Housing types follow that difference. South and West Orange are towns of the kind typically termed "suburban enclaves"; in most of this area, single-family detached houses constitute over 80 percent of the housing stock. By contrast, in much of Orange and East

Fig. 1

● Properties foreclosed on during February 2009
■ Publicly supported development sites

Fig. 2

Population living in poverty

0   5   10   15   20%

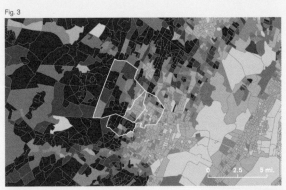

Fig. 3

Housing units that are single-family detached homes

0   20   40   60   80%

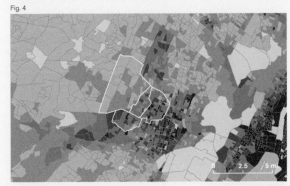

Fig. 4

Commuters who take public transportation to work

0   10   20   30   40%

Orange this housing type amounts to less than 20 percent of the housing stock (fig. 3).

Given the towns' existing transportation infrastructure and links to New York, it is important to highlight the number of commuters in the area who take public transport to work (fig. 4). While that percentage is lower in West Orange than in the other three municipalities, it is still notably higher than the national average of 5 percent.

Local Planning

As the economic bases of the Oranges differ, so too do their local planning strategies. All four have comprehensive development or redevelopment plans in place, but while both Orange and East Orange have designated Urban Enterprise Zones to aid in their economic development, South Orange has enacted a Smart Growth Strategic Plan and West Orange a targeted Neighborhood Preservation Program, among other initiatives.

Possible Sites

Most of the publicly identified development sites in the Oranges are located along the rail line connecting the area to New York (fig. 1 and p. 55).[2] In fact, of the fifteen sites so designated, eight are directly adjacent to this transportation corridor and another two lie within a few blocks of it. Among these are the East Branch of Rahway River Redevelopment in South Orange, three designated Transit Village redevelopment areas in Orange, and the Organon Redevelopment area in West Orange.

1. Sources: U.S. Census Bureau Fact Sheet, "City of Orange township, Essex County, New Jersey: 2005–2009 American Community Survey 5-Year Estimates," http://factfinder.census.gov/servlet/ACSSAFFFacts?_event=Search&geo_id= &_geoContext=&_street=&_county=city+of+orange+township&_cityTown=city+ of+orange+township&_state=04000US34&_zip=&_lang=en&_sse=on&pctxt= fph&pgsl=010. U.S. Census Bureau Fact Sheet, "East Orange city, New Jersey: 2005–2009 American Community Survey 5-Year Estimates," http://factfinder. census.gov/servlet/ACSSAFFFacts?_event=Search&geo_id=&_geoContext=&_ street=&_county=east+orange&_cityTown=east+orange&_state=04000US34&_ zip=&_lang=en&_sse=on&pctxt=fph&pgsl=010. U.S. Census Bureau Fact Sheet, "West Orange township, Essex County, New Jersey: 2005–2009 American Community Survey 5-Year Estimates," http://factfinder.census.gov/servlet/ ACSSAFFFacts?_event=Search&geo_id=&_geoContext=&_street=&_ county=west+orange+township&_cityTown=west+orange+township&_ state=04000US34&_zip=&_lang=en&_sse=on&pctxt=fph&pgsl=010. U.S. Census Bureau Fact Sheet, "South Orange Village township, Essex County, New Jersey: 2005–2009 American Community Survey 5-Year Estimates," http:// factfinder.census.gov/servlet/ACSSAFFFacts?_event=Search&geo_id=&_ geoContext=&_street=&_county=South+Orange+Village+Township&_cityTown =South+Orange+Village+Township&_state=04000US34&_zip=&_lang=en&_ sse=on&pctxt=fph&pgsl=010.
2. See Donald Meisel, "The City of Orange Township: Central Orange Redevelopment Plan (CORP)," November 17, 2003, revised and amended 2009 and 2011, http://www.ci.orange.nj.us/Central_Orange_Redev_Plan.pdf. State of New Jersey Department of Transportation, "Transit Village Initiative: Overview," http:// www.state.nj.us/transportation/community/village/index.shtml. The Cecil Group Team, "South Orange Downtown Vision Plan," Township of South Orange Village, November 2009, http://southorange.org/vision/files/SODowntownVisionPlan- Nov2009(low-res).pdf. The Metro Company, LLC, "Organon Redevelopment Plan," Township of West Orange, New Jersey, July 27, 2006, http://www.westorange.org/ vertical/Sites/%7B8A554F92-3545-4CD9-932E-F8D91F1C9B8B%7D/ uploads/%7B97B3B766-30D6-4DDD-B8B1-3AC3F3DD4499%7D.PDF.

Architectural model of MOS's Thoughts on a Walking City project for Orange, New Jersey, showing the proposed mixed-use development in white filling the street spaces between the existing buildings in blue. All visual materials in this section produced by MOS.

MOS
ARCHITECTS

THOUGHTS
ON A
WALKING CITY

Orange, New Jersey, is a suburb at once of New York City and of Newark. Like many older commuting suburbs on the East Coast, it is well served by regional transit, notably New Jersey Transit, which runs both trains and buses. The Orange rail station lies at the very center of the site chosen for study by MOS Architects and their team, which included expertise in architecture, structural engineering, climate engineering, landscape design, housing policy, economics, and public health. For the last several years the township of the Oranges (which includes East Orange, South Orange, and West Orange as well as the City of Orange studied here) has been studying the creation of three "Transit Villages" to promote mixed-use development within a half-mile, walkable radius from an existing rail station. Despite Orange's accessibility—commuting time to New York averages twenty-five minutes by car or forty minutes by train—there is a significant rate of foreclosure there, and a high rate of unemployment. Tasked in *Foreclosed* with creating a project that might meet local needs but also provide a model with wider applicability, MOS's team undertook an in-depth analysis that considered aspects of municipal budget and infrastructure, public health, and new models of ownership to promote flexibility and diversity, a range of issues extending far beyond those generally considered in isolated development schemes.

Some 15 percent of the land within that half-mile radius of the Orange train station is publicly owned, either as municipal property, in buildings such as schools, or as vacant lots. In addition, some 22 percent of the site is occupied by public streets and sidewalks, laid out in a traditional gridded town plan. Having calculated the annual maintenance expenses that the street infrastructure entails for the municipal budget—an estimated $642,958—MOS proposes the radical gesture of eliminating many of these streets/expenses and replacing them with new, three-story-high, mixed-use structures offering a mixture of commercial, office, and residential spaces, the latter including different apartment types that might be used for a variety of work/live situations. Indeed, much of these new ribbons of building, which would rewrite both the physical and the social space of Orange's center, would be developed as public housing. This kind of flexibility corresponds well to the way many live today, but is currently prevented by most zoning codes and town regulations, including those of Orange. The proposal is intended to reduce the tax burden on an economically challenged city and to redevelop the street as a new economic engine.

This radical new form of urbanism and architectural occupation of the street (something MOS argues has become only a notionally public space, largely given over to private parking, poorly maintained infrastructure, traffic, and private utility companies—a generally dangerous and illegal space for pedestrians to occupy

Above and p. 59: Orange, New Jersey. 2011.

or congregate) is made possible by a form of cooperative ownership, creating a system of portable mortgages where ownership and property are not necessarily assigned to one another. MOS principals Michael Meredith and Hilary Sample describe it as "a kind of micro-governmental cooperative structure, where the local residents participate directly in determining the qualities of their neighborhood."

Unlike earlier urban-renewal models that proposed a wholesale renewal of a site, MOS's project allows the existing and the new to coexist. Orange's streets of largely wood-frame single-family houses are allowed to remain, establishing unexpected juxtapositions with the new ribbon development. This would create a rich variety of spaces and relationships, especially since the ground floors of the new developments might contain a variety of shops and services of use to all residents and neighbors. The future of the existing urban fabric remains one of the puzzling unknowns of this simultaneously poetic and pragmatic project. (Will the abandoned buildings, failing infrastructure, and foreclosed-on houses continue to decay into ruins, or will they be rehabilitated and renewed, or perhaps something in-between?) The MOS proposal creates a set of "cathartic spaces" in quest of "an alternative model of urbanity," using film and photographic simulations to represent an alternate ontology that works as much on the collective imaginary as on models of private property. As the architects explain their larger goal,

> The American model of urbanism is a market-driven collection of discrete enclaves, constructed as an archipelago of distinct lifestyles that are simultaneously connected and disconnected by intricate hierarchies of roads and highways. The poor, and lower middle class, are fundamentally excluded from this model and are thus relegated to their own enclave: the ghetto enclave, the self-perpetuating alter ego of the lifestyle-enclave. This current model is failing us both from a public health (obesity) and energy consumption perspective. We are aiming to find another model of housing and infrastructure where our concept of the public and of freedom isn't based upon the car and highway system.

Statewide Power

NJ has the fifth highest energy costs in the nation after Hawaii, Connecticut, New York and Alaska, paying an average of 16.38 cents per kWh.

Energy costs are higher in NJ because of the state's high-density population and the cost to produce energy with the methods available in-state.

Approximately 40% of the state's energy is imported from neighboring states that are more likely to be associated with carbon-intensive sources, specifically coal.

Essex County
Existing Generation

Proposed Public-Based Micro-Generation

Fuel Type
- Natural Gas / Cogeneration
- Hydro
- Solar
- Wind
- Nuclear
- Biomass or Landfill Gas
- Other fuel sources

Plant type
- Utility
- Industrial
- University Campus
- Distributed Generation

Deregulation to Decentralization

Twenty years ago, long-held perceptions about electricity began to shift. Once viewed as an essential public service, it became viewed as a commodity. This shift is marked by the Energy Policy Act of 1992, which deregulated electricity, allowing it to be traded over wide geographic areas, known as long-distance wheeling, to the highest bidder. The policy was based on the assumption that competition in a free market would keep prices low. The results, however, have been less than ideal.

*Rates have gone up steadily since 2000 in deregulated states.

*No incentive to build new power plants as supply shortages actually drive prices up.

*Transmission-line congestion has increased significantly, contributing to more frequent blackouts.

*Transporting electricity over long distances is inefficient. Wheeling losses result in 10% inefficiency.

By creating a distributed-generation network, service becomes more reliable, more efficient, and less expensive. As a primary element of a public housing development, this model would restore energy as both a public amenity and a public responsibility.

Centralized Generation

In a centralized model, a conventional plant produces large amounts of electricity which are then transmitted over long distances.

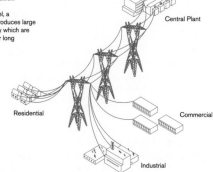

Distributed Generation

With distributed generation, smaller generation facilities service buildings within a local network. These micro-generators can be tied into the utility grid for increased flexibility.

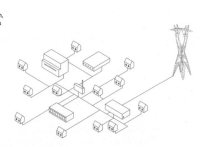

New Jersey Energy

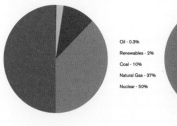

NJ Energy Generation by Fuel Type

Oil · 0.3%

Renewables · 2%

Coal · 10%

Natural Gas · 37%

Nuclear · 50%

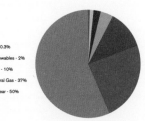

Existing Capacity (in Megawatts) in NJ by Fuel Type

Solar · 2 MW

Solid Waste · 142 MW

Hydro · 405 MW

Diesel · 630 MW

Coal · 2,036 MW

Nuclear · 4,108 MW

Natural Gas · 9,756 MW

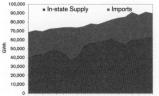

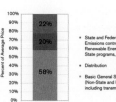

- State and Federal Policy · Emissions control programs, Renewable Energy Development, State programs, etc.
- Distribution
- Basic General Services (Non-State and Federal, including transmission)

Diagram analyzing the energy infrastructure in New Jersey.

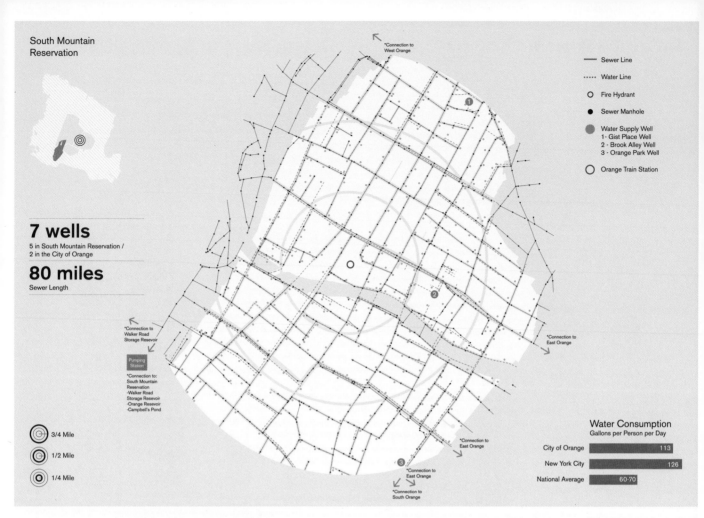

South Mountain
Reservation

7 wells
5 in South Mountain Reservation /
2 in the City of Orange

80 miles
Sewer Length

Sewer Line
Water Line
○ Fire Hydrant
● Sewer Manhole
⬤ Water Supply Well
1- Gist Place Well
2 - Brook Alley Well
3 - Orange Park Well
○ Orange Train Station

*Connection to
West Orange

*Connection to
Walker Road
Storage Resevoir

Pumping
Station

*Connection to:
South Mountain
Reservation
-Walker Road
Storage Resevoir
-Orange Reservoir
-Campbell's Pond

*Connection to
East Orange

*Connection to
East Orange

*Connection to
East Orange

*Connection to
South Orange

3/4 Mile
1/2 Mile
1/4 Mile

Water Consumption
Gallons per Person per Day

City of Orange	113
New York City	126
National Average	60-70

Utilities - Water Infrastructure

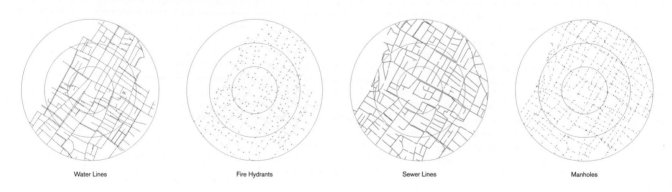

Water Lines   Fire Hydrants   Sewer Lines   Manholes

Diagram analyzing the water infrastructure in the project site.

Transit Station - Walking Radius
From Orange Station, NJ Transit

1/2 Mile

1/4 Mile

1/2 Mile -
10 Minutes

1/4 Mile -
5 Minutes

Diagram showing walking distances and times from the train station.

Site model, plan view.

Left and p. 63: stills from *MOSDrift Orange Edition*, a digital animation produced as part of the project, showing th growth of the units to fill the streets around the station.

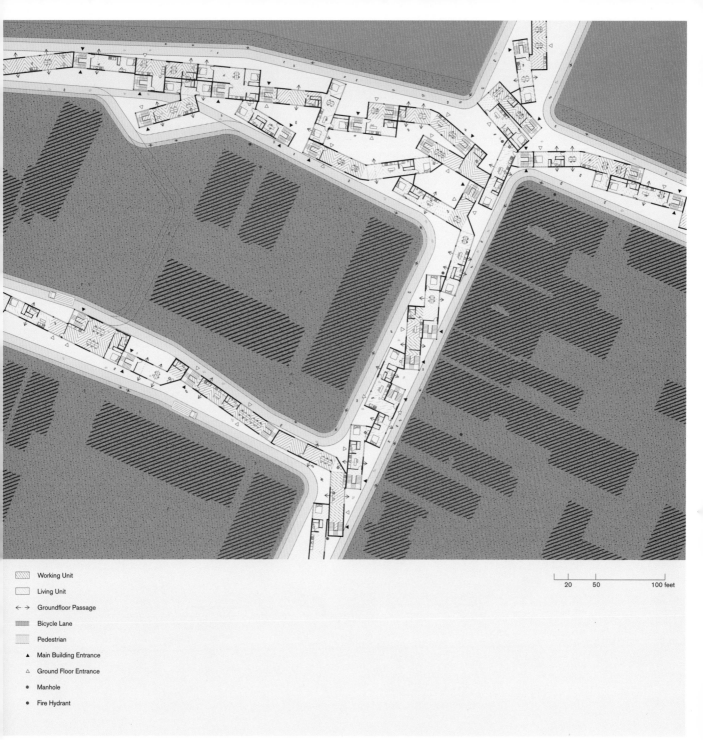

▨	Working Unit
▢	Living Unit
← →	Groundfloor Passage
▨	Bicycle Lane
▨	Pedestrian
▲	Main Building Entrance
△	Ground Floor Entrance
●	Manhole
●	Fire Hydrant

20   50   100 feet

Site plan.

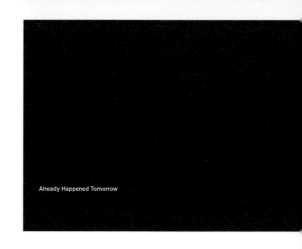

Already Happened Tomorrow

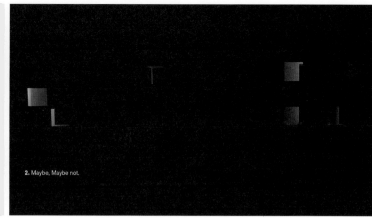

2. Maybe, Maybe not.

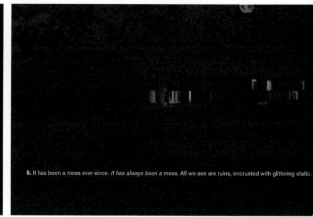

5. It has been a mess ever since. *It has always been a mess.* All we see are ruins, encrusted with glittering static.

Architectural model, showing the mixed-use development between existing houses and industrial buildings.

8. The conversation flipped, the Left/Right poles reversed themselves: On and Off and On and Off, etc... The oscillation was faster and faster until it was On and Off at the same time. The indifference went humming along - assured, if not always smooth - for years and years.

1. *Have you noticed, when someone is really looking at something they become paralyzed for a moment. For mo[st] nothing worse, nothing more embarrassing or humiliating, than being caught in this state.*

6. Parallel Entropies, simultaneity, whatever. If you just wait long enough, at the exact right moment, these entropies align and give the illusion of a grand order. But most of the time we are all just standing around, not really looking at each other, waiting for something to break.

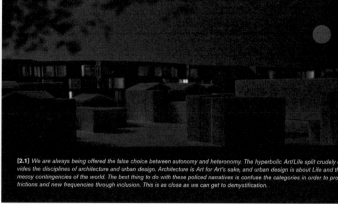

[2.1] We are always being offered the false choice between autonomy and heteronomy. The hyperbolic Art/Life split crudely vides the disciplines of architecture and urban design. Architecture is Art for Art's sake, and urban design is about Life and th messy contingencies of the world. The best thing to do with these policed narratives is confuse the categories in order to pro frictions and new frequencies through inclusion. This is as close as we can get to demystification.

Rendering. To achieve a more efficient infrastructure, individual buildings are connected around shared nodes of building services (stairs, plumbing, service cores).

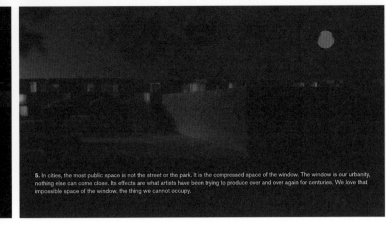

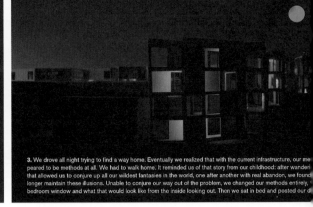

5. In cities, the most public space is not the street or the park. It is the compressed space of the window. The window is our urbanity, nothing else can come close. Its effects are what artists have been trying to produce over and over again for centuries. We love that impossible space of the window, the thing we cannot occupy.

3. We drove all night trying to find a way home. Eventually we realized that with the current infrastructure, our me peared to be methods at all. We had to walk home. It reminded us of that story from our childhood: after wanderi that allowed us to conjure up all our wildest fantasies in the world, one after another with real abandon, we found longer maintain these illusions. Unable to conjure our way out of the problem, we changed our methods entirely, bedroom window and what that would look like from the inside looking out. Then we sat in bed and posted our d

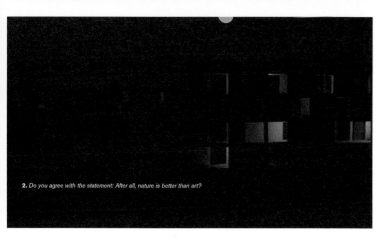

2. *Do you agree with the statement: After all, nature is better than art?*

Left and pp. 66–69: stills from *Already Happened Tomorrow*, a video produced as part of the project.

Rendering. Pedestrian and bicycle passage between new and existing structures.

Questions for the Teams
Michael Meredith and Hilary Sample

What aspects of *The Buell Hypothesis* helped you to frame your project? In what ways do you depart from *The Buell Hypothesis,* and why?

The Buell Hypothesis disputes the notions, first, that there is such a thing as a "typical" American suburb, and second, that in the American context there is such a thing as cohesive public space, suggesting instead that there are "overlapping public spheres." While both of these propositions are accurate approximations of the suburban condition, the suburbs remain the very representation of the "typical." If, as *The Buell Hypothesis* suggests, they were truly exceptional, there would be no point to this exhibition.

The dream of home ownership—of establishing an autonomous and private space—is the attitude out of which the suburbs were produced. If the *Hypothesis* is urging us to change the city by rewriting this narrative of the American Dream, however, then our project has not been entirely faithful to it. Instead of trying to ameliorate the situation through the platitudes of "public space," or by conceiving of a new suburban fantasy (think of gnomes, knolls, fairy tales, and the endlessly bucolic eroticism used to brand suburbia), we've chosen to reimagine the suburb by operating on the proliferation of streets that divide us from our neighbors. The American public sphere has always been a contest among private spheres, a moment of territorial boundaries rather than spaces. Our project occupies and amplifies those lines.

The United States has no tradition of making collective, cathartic spaces as part of the suburban fabric. Here, the public sphere is located in the boundaries between competing private spheres. Rather than change this American Dream, we examine its tenets and utilize its characteristics in order to find an alternate model of urbanity.

How would you describe the interaction of housing, infrastructure, and urbanism in your project?

Whether we approach our urban infrastructure from the perspective of economic viability, environmental impact, or personal health, it no longer serves us well. The public-health concerns that once drove the development of our zoning policies to produce concentrically organized sprawl—in order to separate polluting industry from housing—have created an equally unhealthy environment. A suburbia envisioned as a fix for the harms of the urban setting has instead produced many pressing public-health concerns, from obesity to the stress of isolation. The freedom offered by the automobile has enabled endless sprawl and a sedentary life-style.

For all these reasons, it has become imperative to radically reimagine our small-scale urban centers instead of the peripheries of our cities and towns. Suburbia isn't an isolated problem; our entire mode of urban development needs to be rethought. Our American model of urbanism is a market-driven collection of discrete enclaves, constructed as an archipelago of distinct life-styles that are simultaneously connected and disconnected by intricate hierarchies of roads and highways. This archipelago model of development has produced an underused, inefficient infrastructure and engendered a politics of disengagement. It should be abandoned. In a shift from macro to micro, infrastructure needs to be integrated into our building projects rather than the other way around—needs to become an architectural issue that can be tailored to local engagement, maintenance, and resource management.

It is not a stretch to suggest that our desire for a mythical "freedom" has played a large part in expanding our suburbs, whose domestic separation from the city and among neighbors must be underwritten by massive investments in infrastructure projects, from interstate highways to power lines. Although each of us, as taxpayers, contributes toward our shared infrastructure, the relationship between the individual and the collective has become abstract and broken, to the point where narratives toward the construction of a collective public have been undermined by heroic narratives of individualism. Paradoxically, our nationalist identity (the so-called American Dream) seems more bound to individual freedom than to the collective good. This current rift between the individual's desire and the collective's needs seems irreconcilable. Recognizing this, our proposal envisions a collective urbanism emerging only through an aggregation of small parts—one small building after another. A frontal assault—through a top-down investment in infrastructure, or a challenge to deep-seated belief systems—will be ineffective in reshaping our built environment. If ownership is the driving desire of American development, then our infrastructure should be a vehicle for a new model of ownership. In other words, rather than the *tragedy of the commons,* we opt for the *comedy of the individual.*

How does this project depart from your practice to date? How did you interact with the nondesigner members of your team? What additional expertise do you now wish you might have had as integral to your work, if any?

Most would agree that we were perhaps the oddest choice for this workshop. We were outsiders from the beginning, and as such, we compiled an incredible team of expert consultants—the economist Ed Glaeser, the climate engineers Atelier Ten, the structural engineers AKT, the landscape architects Stoss, the housing policy expert Eric Belsky. Unfortunately there were too many conversations with each of our team members to chronicle here. That said, we hope that there was some value to the disciplines of urban design and planning in our being outsiders. Much of the problem of the suburbs is the result of either too little or too much planning, and as architects with some degree of naivety about the complicated structural issues at hand, we could design a project that breaks free from the top-down-versus-grass-roots dichotomy that brings many policy and design debates to a standstill. We believe that architects have the capacity to engage in the unscripted narratives of a city and to project alternatives that spur the imagination in ways that planning sometimes cannot.

What aspects of your project are specific to your site or suburban municipality? What aspects could be extended to other sites across the country?

Our project emerged from the fact that our site is a transit hub twenty minutes from New York City. Our development model could be adapted anywhere that serves as this kind of transportation center in proximity to a metropolitan area. It could also be applied to other places that could consider reworking the infrastructure of their underutilized streets.

Also, our general engagement with the narrative of suburbia can be readily transposed. We've been told that living in dense cities is the most responsible option, yet we have found that the kinds of desires that lead us to live as we do are rarely about collective responsibility; the dominant way we have tried to instantiate the American Dream has led us to the brink of crisis. Rather than oppose these desires—however irresponsible—our response is to inhabit them in new ways. One example is our project's treatment of private space by exposing it directly to the street through a "window." Where in existing suburban models public space is collapsed into the thin, two-way surface of the window—which often looks onto empty parlors or other unused spaces—our approach toward windows exacerbates the relationship between the private and public spheres to the point at which the window can be claimed as a legitimate space in itself. We've enlarged and repeated the window as a recognizable unit of space because we believe that the space of the window (where the individual and the collective confront each other) is central to our urbanity, and to our identity as individuals within a collective.

On the other hand, while we can imagine some aspects of our project being repeated in other sites, we don't believe that the "suburbs" as a coherent entity can be "solved" through an urban panacea. What we need is to engender a more fundamental shift in our societal values.

How might you use this workshop as a teaching tool?

Architecture has always had a complicated and intertwined relationship to pedagogy and its institutions. Over the past decade, architecture pedagogy has in many ways focused primarily on techniques, and while we could provide a technique-based narrative of our project—utilizing our physics-based software to produce a sort of noncompositional entropic informality—that singular description seems less interesting to us at this moment. Instead, all of the projects in this workshop offer an example of the complex simultaneity of narratives in architecture, illustrating the relationship between political-economic narratives and formal ones, or perhaps between narrative(s) and form more generally. Each project inevitably brings a politics to bear on its architectural aesthetics. This exhibition allows us as architects to oscillate between autonomy and heteronomy, rather than choose between them, in order to find new frictions and frequencies for our work, hopefully enfranchising its audience.

TEMPLE
TERRACE
FLA.

0   1   2 mi.

Simultaneous City project

Temple Terrace municipal boundary
Publicly supported development sites
Simultaneous City area of influence

Temple Terrace, in Hillsborough County, Florida, is a sub-urban area set between Interstate 75, to the east, and the city of Tampa, to the west and south, with which it shares a border and to which its history and its development are tied. Temple Terrace was selected as a case study for *The Buell Hypothesis* not only because analysis showed potential housing need there but also because the town has established redevelopment and revitalization plans, governed by a master plan that includes a form-based code for its downtown core.[1] It is also located within ten miles of a proposed high-speed rail line, one of the criteria for the case study areas. It has no rail station itself, but the existence of public transportation (HART, a local bus network), and the possibility of that network's expansion, render the area representative of many sub-urban settings throughout the country.

Local Economy

Temple Terrace's economy, like that of most of Hillsborough County, is largely tied to Tampa's. Its major industries include tourism, services, and finance, as well as the military—Tampa's MacDill Air Force Base is home to U.S. Central Command. In addition to those directly employed by the armed forces, 17 percent of Temple Terrace's civilian work force hold government jobs.

The foreclosures in and around Temple Terrace in February 2009 (fig. 1) were clustered in the more resi-dential areas in or near Tampa, including some built during the past decade.

Local Conditions

Population densities in Tampa (fig. 2) show that the city is not developed much more densely than surrounding suburbs such as Temple Terrace. (Today this is true of many metropolitan centers in the country.) The percent-age of housing units that are single-family detached houses correlates with the relatively low population density (fig. 3). In much of Tampa, Temple Terrace, and the surrounding area, more than 80 percent of the hous-ing units are single-family detached houses. The U.S. national average is only 61 percent.

This pattern of low-density residential develop-ment affects life-style variables such as commute times. In much of the Tampa area, including parts of Temple Terrace, the proportion of commuters who travel for more than an hour to get to work totals over 20 percent of the commuting work force (fig. 4), as compared with the national mean commute time of 25 minutes.

Local Planning

Local planning in Temple Terrace is currently guided by the master plan, a New Urbanist–inspired proposal developed by Torti Gallas and Partners in 2004. Planning elsewhere in Hillsborough County, including Tampa, includes the redevelopment of former public housing.

Fig. 1

○ Properties foreclosed on during February 2009
▪ Publicly supported development sites

Fig. 2

Population per square mile

0   2.5   5   7.5   10K

Fig. 3

Housing units that are single-family detached homes

0   20   40   60   80%

Fig. 4

Commuters with commutes over 60 minutes

0   5   10   15   20%

Possible Sites

The eight areas marked for public development and chosen as *Buell Hypothesis* case-study sites (fig. 1 and p. 73) span from Temple Terrace toward downtown Tampa, close to the planned high-speed rail station. They range from land formerly used for public services (such as a police station) to vacant land marked for future residential use.[2] Among these are the Temple Terrace Downtown Redevelopment mixed-use zone and, beyond the town line, the now-demolished Central Park Village public housing site.

1. Sources: U.S. Census Bureau Fact Sheet, "Temple Terrace city, Florida: 2005–2009 American Community Survey 5-Year Estimates," online at http://factfinder.census.gov/servlet/ACSSAFFFacts?_event=Search&geo_id=&_geoContext=&_street=&_county=temple+terrace&_cityTown=temple+terrace&_state=04000US12&_zip=&_lang=en&_sse=on&pctxt=fph&pgsl=010.

2. City of Temple Terrace Community Development Department, "Community Redevelopment Area Boundary Map," http://www.templeterrace.com/revitalize/pdfs/CRAmap_033007.pdf. City of Temple Terrace Code of Ordinances, "Chapter 29—Temple Terrace Downtown Community Redevelopment Plan Overlay Zoning District," November 22, 2006, http://www.templeterrace.com/govt/codebook/Chapter%2029.pdf. WilsonMiller, Inc., and Hillsborough County City-County Planning Commission, "Central Park Community Redevelopment Area Plan," May 2006, City of Tampa Economic and Urban Development Department, http://www.tampagov.net/dept_economic_and_urban_development/files/CRA_PLANS/CP_CRAPlan_ApprovedByPC_May22.pdf. Lyman Davidson Dooley, Inc., and the Vlass Group, "Downtown Temple Terrace Site Plan," October 14, 2008, http://www.templeterrace.com/revitalize/pdfs/VlassSitePlan(1).pdf. The Planning Commission, "Adopted 2025 Future Land Use: Unincorporated Hillsborough County," June 2008, http://www.theplanningcommission.org/maps/adoptedpdfmaps/adoptedpdfmaps/AdoptedMaps/Adopted_Tampa_Flu.pdf/view.

Rendering of Visible Weather's Simultaneous City project for Temple Terrace, Florida. All visual materials in this section produced by Visible Weather.

VISIBLE WEATHER

SIMULTANE-OUS CITY

Temple Terrace, Florida. 2011.

Temple Terrace has been something of a suburban experiment since the 1920s, when a ranch belonging to the family of the legendary Chicago businessman Potter Palmer was transformed into a hybrid incorporated city and corporate orange grove. Purchasers of building lots here were also granted stock in the orange grove, and vice versa; the geometry of the grove is still legible in the street pattern. Since the mid-2000s, Temple Terrace has been working to create a New Urbanist "downtown"—something it has never really had—through a public/private partnership to redevelop 225 acres around a major intersection near the city's southwestern border with neighboring Tampa. Development is underway on twenty-nine of these acres, and retail property that the city has purchased—a public investment of around $16 million—has been resold to the designated developer, the Vlass Group.

Asked to study this low-density city/suburb of primarily single-family houses for *Foreclosed*, the New York architectural firm Visible Weather, led by Michael Bell and Eunjeong Seong, formed an interdisciplinary team to suggest alternative planning and financial strategies. The team proposed a different site, focused not on the intersection but on the commercial strip of 56th Street. This two-mile-long site, which parallels the town's border with Tampa, has the same acreage as the planned redevelopment but reconfigures it, weaving together the twenty-nine acres already in process with the underused set-backs, rights of way, parking lots, and sidewalks that are ubiquitous in suburban zoning.

The project, Simultaneous City, would be made possible by the creation of a Real Estate Investment Trust (REIT) to replace the public/private partnership, with an important difference: publicly owned land would remain a public asset, and the income from the development would be shared with citizens. REITs operate by selling stock in their portfolios of real estate. In this case the REIT would be local and public; its income- and investment-generating capacities would serve the immediate community. Simultaneous City provides for a population increase of more than 10,000 people in Temple Terrace; the city's own internal growth is expected to be relatively low, but the project allows it to reap the benefits of growth in its immediate neighbors—Tampa and, to the north, the area around the University of South Florida. Also, the new, linear town center is designed to ease a daily life led without recourse to cars. Its north-south axis would both link the university to the Hillsborough River, a major scenic and recreational feature locally, and provide a development zone for a new, high-efficiency central power plant.

Simultaneous City parallels the existing geographic infrastructure of Temple Terrace while also proposing new financial, structural, and environmental engineering. Central to the project is a mixed-use development, ten times denser than the streets of single-family homes to the east, integrating spaces for city government, municipally owned "incubator" offices for business startups, and three different forms of housing. Here, many trips elsewhere made by car would be possible on foot or by bicycle. Productively blurring the lines between public and private, rental and owned, residential and commercial, the development consists of thin, slablike buildings—one of them a single seventeen-acre block—with a complex multilayered infrastructure. Their construction involves a daringly engineered system of lightweight but rigid structural elements: by setting these elements in tension within a continuous network, the system uses less material then conventional framing, yet is able to span large expanses.

In addition to providing an experientially open large-scale infrastructure, the project specifically addresses the Florida climate. Glazed surfaces would open views to the north, shielding the interiors from southern and western sun. The upper level of the main structure would host a network of courtyard houses, each entered through a garden from an open-air series of corridors and public plazas. These houses offer the same kind of indoor/outdoor living long sought in suburbs but combine it with more-efficient scale and energy use. Each house is divided into vertical zones; living spaces are designed to harvest the dehumidifying prevailing winds, while bedrooms are situated a half level down, protecting them from the heat. The bedrooms are fully conditioned "Cool-Cores," as are those in floor-through apartments at the north end of the complex. These dwelling units are designed to use as little as 30 percent of the energy needs of the average existing house. The entire complex is linked by interwoven walking paths, intended both to build community and to facilitate an environmentally friendly pedestrian life-style.

As Bell and Seong note, "Any small city could use this model to develop underutilized space that is already publicly held: it means that the city would hold property as public and take more control over public investment in the property." Here the disappearance from suburbia of the civic amenities that are commonly provided by larger cities, and often featured in developer suburbs of earlier decades, are made possible by a novel experiment in channeling profit and equity toward public ownership. "The collective income of Temple Terrace," Visible Weather notes, "with an additional 10,000 residents could fund a dramatically higher quality of housing and investment in housing." Where existing suburban models "atomize this financial power into single-family houses that receive little or no engineering or design expertise," this model would leverage the power of the collective while providing a privacy, independence, and environmental performance far exceeding the standard today.

Reverse Engineering Temple Terrace Development Mode

Temple Terrace	
6.9	sq. miles
192,360,960	sq.ft.
4,416	acres
24,541	Population
5.56	Density (People Per Acre)
10,093	Housing Units
2.431487169	Household Size
2,200	Avg. House Size (sq.ft.)
22,204,600	Residential (sq.ft.)
0.23	Housing Units Per Acre
3,364	Model Residential Square Feet
0.077234466	Model Housing Units Per Acre

Assumptions		
Relative Density Multiple:		3.(
Residential (% of Development)		55%
Commercial (% of Development)		45.0%
Avg. Residential Dvlp. Costs PSF		$300
Avg. Non-Residential Dvlp. Costs PSF		$300
Loss Percentage		15.00%
Parking Bay Size	(sq.ft.)	15(
Parking Ratio (1:X)	(sq.ft.)	200(

Variable Selection/Input

33 Acres_x3 (Density Multiple)

Development Capacity Model

CRA Density		Acres	Gross Devp. Sq. Ft.	Parking (sq.ft.)	Parking Spaces	Net. Devp. Sq. Ft.	Residential Units (Total)	New Resident Population	Aver
FAR	1.00	33	1,437,480	107,811	719	1,329,669	185	449	
FAR	1.50		2,156,220	161,717	1,078	1,994,504	326	793	
FAR	2.00		2,874,960	215,622	1,437	2,659,338	435	1,057	
FAR	2.50		3,593,700	269,528	1,797	3,324,173	543	1,321	
FAR	3.00		4,312,440	323,433	2,156	3,989,007	652	1,586	
FAR	3.50		5,031,180	377,339	2,516	4,653,842	761	1,850	
FAR	4.00		5,749,920	431,244	2,875	5,318,676	869	2,114	
FAR	4.50		6,468,660	485,150	3,234	5,983,511	978	2,378	
FAR	5.00		7,187,400	539,055	3,594	6,648,345	1,087	2,643	
FAR	5.50		7,906,140	592,961	3,953	7,313,180	1,196	2,907	
FAR	6.00		8,624,880	646,866	4,312	7,978,014	1,304	3,171	
FAR	6.50		9,343,620	700,772	4,672	8,642,849	1,413	3,436	
FAR	7.00		10,062,360	754,677	5,031	9,307,683	1,522	3,700	

Development Pro-Forma (Rented Units)

FAR	Total Development Cost	Equity	Debt	Annual Debt Service	Ad Valorem Revenue	Housing Rental Revenue
1.00	$190,799,543.81	$19,079,954.38	$171,719,589.43	($13,737,580.39)	$1,171,299.32	$15,609,178.45
1.50	$289,188,964.52	$28,918,896.45	$260,270,068.07	($20,821,625.50)	$1,775,302.13	$27,545,609.02
2.00	$385,585,286.02	$38,558,528.60	$347,026,757.42	($27,762,167.33)	$2,367,069.51	$36,727,478.70
2.50	$481,981,607.53	$48,198,160.75	$433,783,446.78	($34,702,709.17)	$2,958,836.89	$45,909,348.37
3.00	$578,377,929.03	$57,837,792.90	$520,540,136.13	($41,643,251.00)	$3,550,604.27	$55,091,218.05
3.50	$674,774,250.54	$67,477,425.05	$607,296,825.49	($48,583,792.84)	$4,142,371.65	$64,273,087.72
4.00	$771,170,572.05	$77,117,057.20	$694,053,514.84	($55,524,334.67)	$4,734,139.02	$73,454,957.40
4.50	$867,566,893.55	$86,756,689.36	$780,810,204.20	($62,464,876.50)	$5,325,906.40	$82,636,827.07
5.00	$963,963,215.06	$96,396,321.51	$867,566,893.55	($69,405,418.34)	$5,917,673.78	$91,818,696.74
5.50	$1,060,359,536.56	$106,035,953.66	$954,323,582.91	($76,345,960.17)	$6,509,441.16	$101,000,566.42
6.00	$1,156,755,858.07	$115,675,585.81	$1,041,080,272.26	($83,286,502.00)	$7,101,208.54	$110,182,436.09
6.50	$1,253,152,179.57	$125,315,217.96	$1,127,836,961.62	($90,227,043.84)	$7,692,975.92	$119,364,305.77
7.00	$1,349,548,501.08	$134,954,850.11	$1,214,593,650.97	($97,167,585.67)	$8,284,743.29	$128,546,175.44

Infrastructural Impact

Police			Fire/Emergency Medical			Water			Sewer
0.9	officers	$62,896.45	0.9	officers	$89,852.08	16,398,004	gallons/yr	$224,630.19	1
1.6	officers	$110,993.74	1.6	officers	$158,562.49	28,937,654	gallons/yr	$396,406.22	2
2.1	officers	$147,991.66	2.1	officers	$211,416.65	38,583,539	gallons/yr	$528,541.63	2
2.6	officers	$184,989.57	2.6	officers	$264,270.81	48,229,423	gallons/yr	$660,677.03	3
3.2	officers	$221,987.48	3.2	officers	$317,124.98	57,875,308	gallons/yr	$792,812.44	4
3.7	officers	$258,985.40	3.7	officers	$369,979.14	67,521,193	gallons/yr	$924,947.85	5
4.2	officers	$295,983.31	4.2	officers	$422,833.30	77,167,077	gallons/yr	$1,057,083.25	5
4.8	officers	$332,981.22	4.8	officers	$475,687.46	86,812,962	gallons/yr	$1,189,218.66	6
5.3	officers	$369,979.14	5.3	officers	$528,541.63	96,458,847	gallons/yr	$1,321,354.07	7
5.8	officers	$406,977.05	5.8	officers	$581,395.79	106,104,732	gallons/yr	$1,453,489.47	7
6.3	officers	$443,974.97	6.3	officers	$634,249.95	115,750,616	gallons/yr	$1,585,624.88	8
6.9	officers	$480,972.88	6.9	officers	$687,104.11	125,396,501	gallons/yr	$1,717,760.29	9
7.4	officers	$517,970.79	7.4	officers	$739,958.28	135,042,386	gallons/yr	$1,849,895.69	10

4 Acres_x3 (Density Multiple)

Development Capacity Model

CRA Density		Acres	Gross Devp. Sq. Ft.	Parking (sq.ft.)	Parking Spaces	Net. Devp. Sq. Ft.	Residential Units (Total)	New Resident Population	Aver
FAR	1.00	4	174,240	13,068	87	161,172	22	54	
FAR	1.50		261,360	19,602	131	241,758	40	96	
FAR	2.00		348,480	26,136	174	322,344	53	128	
FAR	2.50		435,600	32,670	218	402,930	66	160	
FAR	3.00		522,720	39,204	261	483,516	79	192	
FAR	3.50		609,840	45,738	305	564,102	92	224	
FAR	4.00		696,960	52,272	348	644,688	105	256	
FAR	4.50		784,080	58,806	392	725,274	119	288	
FAR	5.00		871,200	65,340	436	805,860	132	320	
FAR	5.50		958,320	71,874	479	886,446	145	352	
FAR	6.00		1,045,440	78,408	523	967,032	158	384	
FAR	6.50		1,132,560	84,942	566	1,047,618	171	416	
FAR	7.00		1,219,680	91,476	610	1,128,204	184	448	

Development Pro-Forma (Rented Units)

FAR	Total Development Cost	Equity	Debt	Annual Debt Service	Ad Valorem Revenue	Housing Rental Revenue
1.00	$23,127,217.43	$2,312,721.74	$20,814,495.69	($1,665,161.26)	$141,975.68	$1,892,021.63
1.50	$35,053,207.82	$3,505,320.78	$31,547,887.04	($2,523,833.39)	$215,188.14	$3,338,861.70
2.00	$46,737,610.43	$4,673,761.04	$42,063,849.38	($3,365,111.19)	$286,917.52	$4,451,815.60
2.50	$58,422,013.03	$5,842,201.30	$52,579,811.73	($4,206,388.99)	$358,646.90	$5,564,769.50
3.00	$70,106,415.64	$7,010,641.56	$63,095,774.08	($5,047,666.79)	$430,376.27	$6,677,723.40
3.50	$81,790,818.25	$8,179,081.82	$73,611,736.42	($5,888,944.59)	$502,105.65	$7,790,677.30
4.00	$93,475,220.85	$9,347,522.09	$84,127,698.77	($6,730,222.38)	$573,835.03	$8,903,631.20
4.50	$105,159,623.46	$10,515,962.35	$94,643,661.11	($7,571,500.18)	$645,564.41	$10,016,585.10
5.00	$116,844,026.07	$11,684,402.61	$105,159,623.46	($8,412,777.98)	$717,293.79	$11,129,539.00
5.50	$128,528,428.67	$12,852,842.87	$115,675,585.81	($9,254,055.78)	$789,023.17	$12,242,492.90
6.00	$140,212,831.28	$14,021,283.13	$126,191,548.15	($10,095,333.58)	$860,752.55	$13,355,446.80
6.50	$151,897,233.89	$15,189,723.39	$136,707,510.50	($10,936,611.37)	$932,481.93	$14,468,400.70
7.00	$163,581,636.49	$16,358,163.65	$147,223,472.85	($11,777,889.17)	$1,004,211.31	$15,581,354.60

Infrastructural Impact

Police			Fire/Emergency Medical			Water			Sewer
0.1	officers	$7,623.81	0.1	officers	$10,891.16	1,987,637	gallons/yr	$27,227.90	
0.2	officers	$13,453.79	0.2	officers	$19,219.70	3,507,594	gallons/yr	$48,049.24	
0.3	officers	$17,938.38	0.3	officers	$25,626.26	4,676,793	gallons/yr	$64,065.65	
0.3	officers	$22,422.98	0.3	officers	$32,032.83	5,845,991	gallons/yr	$80,082.06	
0.4	officers	$26,907.57	0.4	officers	$38,439.39	7,015,189	gallons/yr	$96,098.48	
0.4	officers	$31,392.17	0.4	officers	$44,845.96	8,184,387	gallons/yr	$112,114.89	
0.5	officers	$35,876.76	0.5	officers	$51,252.52	9,353,585	gallons/yr	$128,131.30	
0.6	officers	$40,361.36	0.6	officers	$57,659.09	10,522,783	gallons/yr	$144,147.72	
0.6	officers	$44,845.96	0.6	officers	$64,065.65	11,691,981	gallons/yr	$160,164.13	
0.7	officers	$49,330.55	0.7	officers	$70,472.22	12,861,180	gallons/yr	$176,180.54	
0.8	officers	$53,815.15	0.8	officers	$76,878.78	14,030,378	gallons/yr	$192,196.96	1
0.8	officers	$58,299.74	0.8	officers	$83,285.35	15,199,576	gallons/yr	$208,213.37	1
0.9	officers	$62,784.34	0.9	officers	$89,691.91	16,368,774	gallons/yr	$224,229.78	1

Economic and spatial model: reverse-engineering the Temple Terrace redevelopment plan.

Infrastructure Unit Cost Assumptions

Facility	Imputed Level of Service		Unit Cost	
Parks and Recreation	5	acres per 1,000 residents	$100,000	acre
Police	2	officers per 1,000 residents	$70,000	officer
Fire/Emergency Medical	2	officers per 1,000 residents	$100,000	officer
Water	100	gallons per capita per day	$5	gallon
Sewer	75	gallons per capita per day	$10	gallon
Stormwater	500	sq. ft. impervious surface per capita	$1	sq. ft.
Public Buildings	0.5	sq. ft. per capita	$300	sq. ft.
Courts and Justice	0.5	sq.ft. per capita	$500	sq. ft.
Libraries	0.5	sq.ft. per capita	$400	sq. ft.
Schools	0.4	students per household	$20,000	student

Income Model Assumptions

Expense/Vacancy/Credit Ratio	50%	
Finance		
	8%	rate
	180	term
	90%	LTC
Program		
Commercial	33%	Retail
	45%	Office
	12%	Civic
Rates	$15	Retail/PSF
	$20	Office/PSF
	$15	Civic/PSF
Housing	80%	Rental
	20%	For Sale
Rates	$12	Rental/PSF
	$120	For Sale/PSF

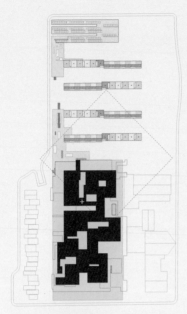

Site Plan + First Level
Temple Terrace City Hall

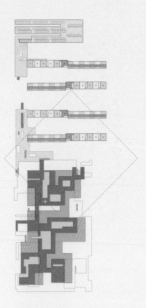

Second Level
Temple Terrace Incubator Office Space (green)

Site Plan + Third Level
Housing and "Streets under the Sky"

1. New Street Crossing North 56th Street: Traffic Slowed by New Paving

2. Courtyard Housing: 1500 sq. ft. with 500 sq. ft. Outdoor Space

3. "Streets under the Sky" / Tensegrity Deck

4. Courtyard and Lightwell to Incubator Office and City Hall

5. Existing Church and Day-Care Facility

6. Roof-Deck Community Space above Local Retail and Commercial Space

7. Entry to Shared Office Spaces and Neighborhood Amenities

8. Floor-Thru Duplex Flats with Cool Core

9. Floor-Thru Flats with Cool Core

10. Health and Social Services

11. Supportive Housing: First Step Housing, Foyer Housing, Veterans' Housing

12. Public Playgrounds for Housing

13. Entry to City Hall

14. Public Plaza Event Space

15. Transit Stops

16. Temple Terrace 2 Mile Linear Park (with Landscape by West 8)

17. Temple Terrace "Block Park" (with Landscape by West 8 and VisibleWeather)

18. Temple Terrace FREE Electric-Car Charging Depots

Floor and site plans.

- ■ City of Temple Terrace, Florida
- □ City of Tampa, Florida
- ▨ Hillsborough County, Florida
- ■ Site
- ▦ Simultaneous City: 225 Acre: New Linear
  High-Density Urban Zone
- ■ Redevelopment Plan as of 2009. 225-Acre
  Public/Private Partnership "Downtown."

Diagram showing the site's location in the border area between Temple Terrace and Tampa.

Rendering of the site, seen from the northwest. Three housing types fuse in a continuous landscape of government, office, and retail services.

Architectural model.

Architectural model.

Architectural model. A diamond-shaped core sample of the mixed-use development.

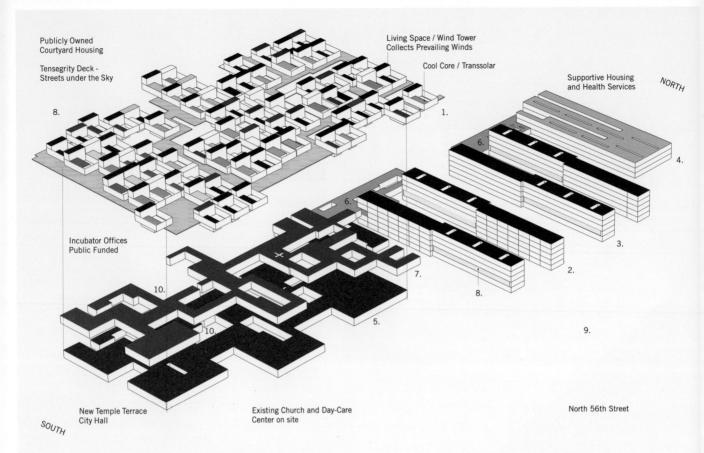

Publicly Owned
Courtyard Housing

Tensegrity Deck -
Streets under the Sky

8.

Living Space / Wind Tower
Collects Prevailing Winds

Cool Core / Transsolar

Supportive Housing
and Health Services

NORTH

1.

6.

4.

6.

3.

2.

7.

8.

Incubator Offices
Public Funded

10.

10.

5.

9.

New Temple Terrace
City Hall

SOUTH

Existing Church and Day-Care
Center on site

North 56th Street

Program Key

1. Tensegrity Structure and Courtyard Housing
Unit count: 80. Unit size: 1500 sq. ft. total:
Interior space is 1000 sq. ft. with two
bedrooms

2. Bar Buildings: Flats with Cool Cores
Unit count: 88. Units size: 34 feet x 20 =
680 sq. ft. with two small bedrooms and two
living spaces for live/work

3. Bar Buildings: Duplex with Cool Cores
Unit count: 56. Unit size: 30 x 34 = 1020 sq.
ft. with two bedrooms

4. Supportive Housing: 50,000 sq. ft.
Unit count: 200 Supportive Housing Units.
First Step Housing / Foyer Housing / Veterans'
Housing. Community Solutions and Common
Ground Community

5. Public Space: Temple Terrace City Hall
40,000 sq. ft.

6. Public Space: Local Retail and Commercial
Space
20,000 sq. ft.

7. Public Space: City of Temple Terrace
Incubator Offices

8. Communal Shared Work Space

9. Public Plaza and Event Spaces, Transit
Depots for Electric-Car Charging Stations, +
New Linear park at North 56th Street

10. Lightwells and Courtyard link Housing,
Office and City Hall programming

Diagram showing intermix of programming.

Rendering, showing public plaza and entry to City Hall with three housing types suspended above.

Rendering, showing the view from communal offices toward a public plaza and City Hall.

Architectural model.

Rendering, showing courtyard houses and view to incubator offices and City Hall below.

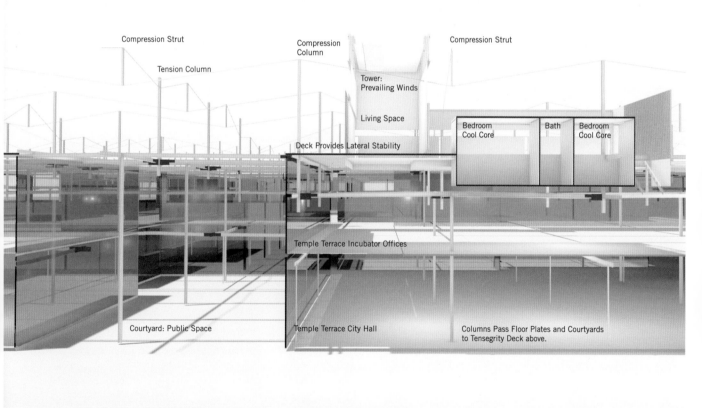

Compression Strut

Tension Column

Compression Column

Compression Strut

Tower: Prevailing Winds

Living Space

Deck Provides Lateral Stability

Bedroom Cool Core

Bath

Bedroom Cool Core

Temple Terrace Incubator Offices

Courtyard: Public Space

Temple Terrace City Hall

Columns Pass Floor Plates and Courtyards to Tensegrity Deck above.

Annotated cross-section, showing integration of program with structural and environmental engineering.

Rendering. The planar structure of the slab buildings combines program and solar protection. Engineering allows new forms of social experience and collective space.

Questions for the Teams
Michael Bell, Eunjeong Seong

What aspects of *The Buell Hypothesis* helped you to frame your project? In what ways do you depart from *The Buell Hypothesis*, and why?

The long-standing debates about the decline of public space, or its simulation within private property, are played out in our project as a populating of publicly mandated but peopleless zoning set-backs along publicly funded roads. We sought to fuse public infrastructure with housing and to curtail normal use segregation in a new publicly held redevelopment. Temple Terrace (or any small city) could use this model to develop underutilized space that is already publicly held: it means that the city would hold property as public and take more control over the collective investment in the property.

How would you describe the interaction of housing, infrastructure, and urbanism in your project?

They are parallel and partially fused. Temple Terrace has no significant mass transit, but it does have a scale that could support walking, bicycling, and electric cars. We designed an aggregation of 225 acres that lines both sides of the city's main artery, 56th Street: the zone would link the University of South Florida with the river to the south, but would also form a new border zone for as many as 10,000 new residents. This zone would form the nucleus for a new mass transit system in the future and over time would become a magnet that could replace the single-family-house community.

How does this project depart from your practice to date? How did you interact with the nondesigner members of your team? What additional expertise do you now wish you might have had as integral to your work, if any?

We've always worked closely with engineers and policy partners. For this project we tried to work with the team at the outset and near simultaneously. It caused a certain amount of confusion, as we had structural details before a program, thermal ideas before a floor plan. Our early presentations at MoMA PS1 suffered from this, but in the end we feel that the engineering and the financial planning became social—that is, they enabled new ways to live, new experiences. There was no lack of expertise but we could have used more time to coordinate expert input: we felt a need to address architectural history in the context of works that took on mass housing in the past—it was a lot to coordinate in a short time, and the workshop aspect of this was at times at odds with the more private role of history and theory.

What aspects of your project are specific to your site or suburban municipality? What aspects could be extended to other sites across the country?

The specific scale of Temple Terrace deeply affected the project, as did its border relation to Tampa. The lack of public transit, and the redevelopment already underway, were explicit and we reacted carefully to them. But the North 56th Street strip and its single-use commercial zoning are of a kind ubiquitous in the United States, as is the low density of 4.5 people per acre. Early on, we produced a "reverse engineering" financial analysis of the Temple Terrace city budget to show how the city's aggregate income and financial capacity could provide greater common good if they could be used to develop a hybridized and high-density form of housing and public building that were fused with the underutilized space of the strip. This was specific to the site but also a reaction to the fact that in the United States, low-density speculative housing carries almost no research or development funding and as such shows little innovation. Spec houses are essentially not designed by architects or engineers; higher-density housing requires more engineering and design, but can also leverage the overall capitalization and financial might of the collective, in ways that the disaggregated housing expenditures of single-family houses can't. Temple Terrace's residents could spend 30 percent of the $700 million they collectively earn annually and remain within HUD housing-cost guidelines, but the disaggregated way in which housing monies are spent means that they are spent on a very low-level commodity. In this way single-family houses essentially thwart the levels of innovation that funding buys in the centralized, highly controlled environments of commodities such as automobiles and computers. We were seeking ways in which housing density could address the privacy and independence people seek in housing but also move housing design into a realm where the funding levels do more to capitalize innovation and aggregate value.

How might you use this workshop as a teaching tool?

The combination of research and design, and also of urbanism and architecture, is common in architecture schools today but is also contentious and unresolved in many ways. A great deal of analysis is done in studios today under the rubrics of economics, demographics, and even finance, but it is framed as a kind of reconnaissance mission: designers are not so much forecasting or shaping a future world as trying to grasp something they feel has eclipsed them and their aspirations. At MoMA PS1 we were trying to grasp a situation (foreclosures, market collapse, regulation of housing), but we also felt a drive to respond with a vision of what could be, a vision not based in a moderated adjudication of the crisis. The workshop's framing of the suburbs as a zone conflating architecture, infrastructure, and social life stands at the forefront of work that will eventually rewrite the geography of American cities. We often think schools have inadvertently created an environment where they appraise often fragmented and incomplete research, and allow an architecture that is too derivative of that process. *Foreclosed* forced us to think about this because, very simply, we didn't want to exhibit research; we wanted to show a proposal. At the same time, the workshop forced an opening to research in very public ways. It was a unique experience and we think a critical part of how this project might affect schools.

CICERO
ILL.

0   0.5   1 mi.

The Garden in the Machine project

---- Cicero municipal boundary
Publicly supported development sites

In the area around the proposed high-speed rail line between Chicago and St. Louis are a variety of municipalities demonstrating housing need or instability, from small rural centers to the older suburbs of Chicago. Cicero, Illinois, is representative of those inner-ring suburbs. It is also relevant for its aggressive approach to the foreclosure crisis.[1]

Local Economy
Cicero lies adjacent to Chicago in Cook County. Local employment is largely in production and transportation (34 percent) and in manufacturing (26 percent). The predominant land use is residential but the town has a small industrial core, flanked on the north and south by the Blue and Pink lines of Chicago's El transit system. Farther to the south, Cicero also has a station on the local Metra rail system.

Foreclosure rates in Cicero continued to rise in 2009 (fig. 1), with officials estimating that over half of the mortgages held by homeowners were subprime high-interest loans.[2]

Local Conditions
Like many older inner-ring suburbs, Cicero is a relatively densely developed residential area (fig. 2). It contains more pockets of small single-family homes than appear in other suburbs in this study.

Similarly, Cicero's high rental rates (fig. 3) make for a closer affinity to Chicago, with its urban renting lifestyle, than to other outlying suburbs. This inner suburb is also at the edge between different income-distribution patterns, separating the lower-income neighborhoods closer to the center of Chicago from the more affluent suburbs to the west (fig. 4).

Local Planning
Local planning and redevelopment advocates in Cicero have taken an aggressive approach to the danger of blight created by high numbers of foreclosed and abandoned properties. The town government, for example, issued a Request for Qualifications for the redevelopment of individual scattered lots. It also generated a Neighborhood Stabilization Program, which calculated the number of residential foreclosures in each census tract and identified target areas for intervention. Then, in 2008, the town followed the steps necessary to take advantage of the Community Development Block Grant program, made available by the American Recovery and Reinvestment Act (ARRA) for infrastructural improvement and economic development.

Possible Sites
The publicly supported development sites in Cicero range in size from the network of individual lots identified by the town to the larger redevelopment of the

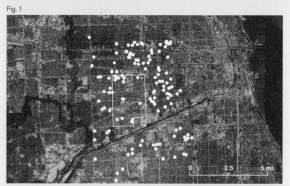

Fig. 1

○ Properties foreclosed on during February 2009
▬ Publicly supported development sites

Fig. 2

Population per square mile

0 10 15 20 25K

Fig. 3

Housing units that are rented

0 20 40 60 80%

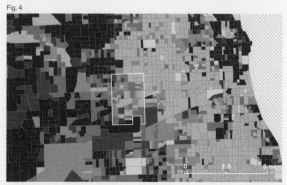

Fig. 4

Median household income

0 35 40 45 $50K

municipally owned former Sportsman's Park racetrack in the southern part of the town (fig. 1 and p. 91).[3] Here also, more explicitly than elsewhere, foreclosed properties represent realizable new sites for the development of housing alongside sites already slated for publicly funded development. Using a fund created by the 2008 Housing and Economic Recovery Act, Cicero has sought to underwrite the purchase and rehabilitation of these foreclosed properties.

1. Sources: U.S. Census Bureau Fact Sheet, "Cicero town, Illinois: 2005–2009 American Community Survey 5-Year Estimates," http://factfinder.census.gov/servlet/ACSSAFFFacts?_event=Search&geo_id=&_geoContext=&_street=&_county=cicero&_cityTown=cicero&_state=04000US17&_zip=&_lang=en&_sse=on&pctxt=fph&pgsl=010.

2. Town of Cicero Department of Housing, "Public Notice. Amendments to Annual Action Plans: Neighborhood Stabilization Program," http://www.thetownofcicero.com/content/img/f226553/2009amendment2.pdf.

3. Town of Cicero, "Notice of Request for Proposal: Sportsman's Park Redevelopment Project," January 30, 2007, http://www.thetownofcicero.com/content/img/f189852/rfp.sportsmanspark.f.1.30.07.pdf. "Request for Proposals for Professional Engineering Services Design and Construction Engineering for Roosevelt Road between Austin Boulevard and Harlem Avenue," August 2008, http://www.thetownofcicero.com/content/img/f215536/RFP_Egineering_Roosevelt_082608.pdf. "Request for Architectural/Engineering/Construction Management Qualifications: Rehabilitation of Vacant and Foreclosed Residential Units under the Neighborhood Stabilization Program," May 2009, http://www.thetownofcicero.com/content/img/f221321/rfq-architectural-services-foreclosed-residential-units-revised052809.pdf.

Rendering of Studio Gang's Garden in the Machine project for Cicero, Illinois. All visual materials in this section produced by Studio Gang.

STUDIO GANG ARCHITECTS

THE GARDEN IN THE MACHINE

Cicero, Illinois. 2011.

Cicero is an aging inner-ring suburb set on the edge of metropolitan Chicago, and along freight rail lines predicted to increase in capacity. Famed for organized crime and civil rights marches in the last century, it has lately become an arrival point for new immigrants to the region, the great majority of them Mexican and Central American. Cicero has experienced a high rate of foreclosure in its fabric of tightly spaced brick bungalows dating from the 1920s and '30s. Built for a previous generation of Czech, Polish, and Lithuanian immigrants, these houses have often been repurposed as multifamily dwellings by more recent residents. Industrial as well as residential properties have faced foreclosure, and a distinctive feature of the proposal of the group led by Jeanne Gang—a Chicago architect much concerned with the dialogue between architecture and both human and natural ecologies—is to interweave responses to both situations.

Gang's team, which included an affordable-housing advocate, urban and landscape designers, a journalist, and an artist/cultural developer, realized that like many inner-ring suburbs around the country, Cicero is facing three challenges: industrial decline, rising unemployment coupled with high poverty rates, and environmental contamination. The team turned these problems into potential opportunities by taking on both the urban fabric of the town and the financial architecture of living and working there. As the team concludes,

> The American Dream has always been about the freedom to remake oneself. America used to support that goal, but now impediments have been put into place. Our project is trying to remove those impediments. The American Dream for new arrivals is not about escaping the city for a rural refuge, it is rather a dream of opportunity, education, starting a business, helping one's children succeed.

To this end the team decided to focus on an unexpected site, a former factory whose adjacency to housing stock allowed them to imagine how new intervention in Cicero might be connected to the town's existing fabric. Inverting the title of the cultural historian Leo Marx's classic book *The Machine in the Garden* (1964), which discussed the conflict between America's pastoral ideal and its industrial ambitions, they propose that lost industry is our legacy and the notion of a garden must be cultivated anew within it, not as a fragment of nature to be viewed in the backyard but as "an integrated system for people and a regional process that will restore land."

The Studio Gang team set out to create new housing types able to mix families and generations, living and working, in ways that are generally prohibited under existing zoning codes. Using the analogy of the Rubik's Cube, the team asked themselves, "What if the bungalow could be taken apart and sorted into separate pieces—bedroom, kitchen, lawns—and reassembled as needed?" They then designed a new kind of "Recombinant House" enabling that flexibility. The house is affordable because people can buy only what they need at the time they need it, and then can add or subtract spaces as families grow, shrink, or otherwise change. Communal spaces can be shared among families, while work spaces will allow people to start businesses—generally informal, entrepreneurial businesses, such as bakeries, repair shops, and light manufacturing. Some of this is made possible by restructuring existing bungalows, but the anchor of the new development is a "vertical neighborhood" that shuffles and stacks homes in flexible combinations tailored to the resident's changing needs. This is achieved by redeploying the construction elements of the abandoned factory, notably its steel trusses, which are repurposed to span the distances between newly built concrete cores containing utilities, allowing for great flexibility within the building framework and for the introduction of open spaces and gardens on multiple levels. At the scale of the urban block, the entire community is also reconfigured zto allow the seamless coexistence of homes, work areas, public amenities, and a variety of green spaces. On a regional scale, these green spaces would align with the abundant rail track to form "wildlife corridors."

Not only would this proposal require legal changes in Cicero, especially in zoning, but it is also posited on a new model of ownership, a "Limited Equity Cooperative" that decouples the ownership of the home from the land below it. Residents still own their spaces, and thus have an incentive to care for them, but the land and shared amenities are owned by a private trust. The trust places a permanent ceiling on the costs (and also on the financial upside) of ownership. Covenants require owners to sell their homes or co-op shares back to the trust. Residents may realize gains from sweat-equity investments in their housing, but they are otherwise shielded from swings in the real estate market, and there is always a ready buyer for their homes. This existing financial model finds an original and highly flexible architectural, urban, and landscape expression in Studio Gang's proposal. Their solution is both specific to Cicero, making the town a machine for the American Dream of new arrivals, and offers a model with broad applicability. "Grass," Gang notes, "the suburb's singular expression of green, is expanded in both variety and scale.... Biodigesters and functional wetlands cleanse the neighborhood's waste water, shaded plazas accommodate public festivals and markets, shared vegetable gardens serve neighboring families, and regionally scaled wildlife corridors support global biodiversity."

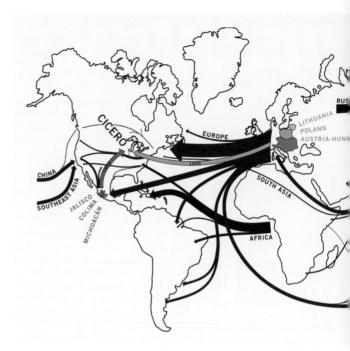

Diagram showing world migrations since 1785. Many inner-ring suburbs like Cicero have become gateways for new immigrants, a role traditionally played by large cities.

Stills from *Cicero Foreclosed*, a film of interviews with Cicero residents produced as part of the project.

RENT FOR OUR HOUSE, OUR CAR

AND THE BUSINESS, IT WAS JUST A LOT

OW WE'RE GOING BACK TO

A SINGLE BUNGALOW

ENTIRE FAMILY UPSTAIRS

THE THING I CAN SAY ABOUT MY CULTURE

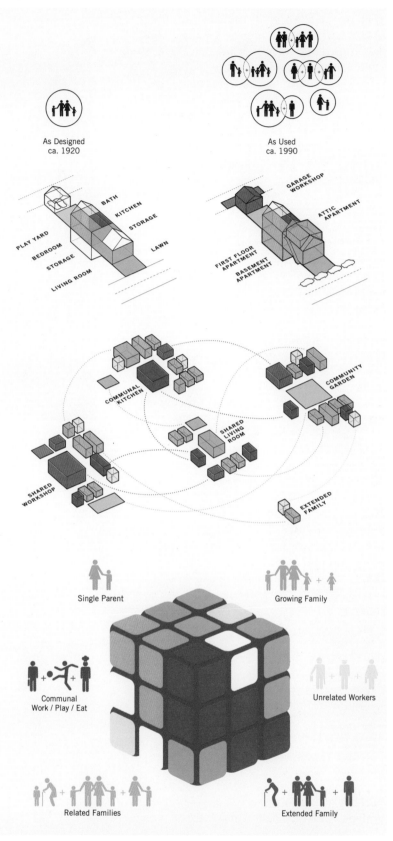

Diagram showing how bungalows built in the 1920s for nuclear families no longer fit Cicero's current residents and are often subdivided into smaller units. The Garden in the Machine project proposes sorting their parts into a new, recombinant housing type that meets the needs of twenty-first-century families.

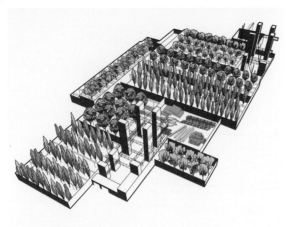

"Born-Again Factory": a foreclosed-upon factory would be transformed by plantings of trees and vegetation to cleanse the soil. As that process continued, the materials of the factory building would be salvaged, sorted, and recycled on-site into components for the new structures.

Poplars, willows, and other phyto-accumulators would cleanse the soil around the former factory in as little as four to five years.

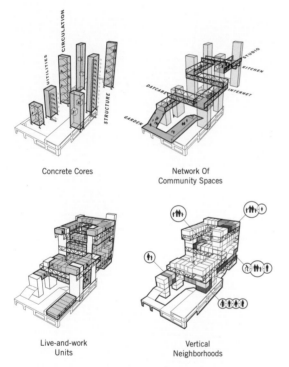

Concrete Cores

Network Of Community Spaces

Live-and-work Units

Vertical Neighborhoods

"Vertical Neighborhoods": the concrete cores of the project's buildings contain utilities and circulation and constitute the primary vertical structure. Reclaimed trusses span the cores, forming a network of community spaces. Private live-and-work units are mounted above and below the trusses. Vertical Neighborhood units can be reconfigured as families come and go, shrink and grow.

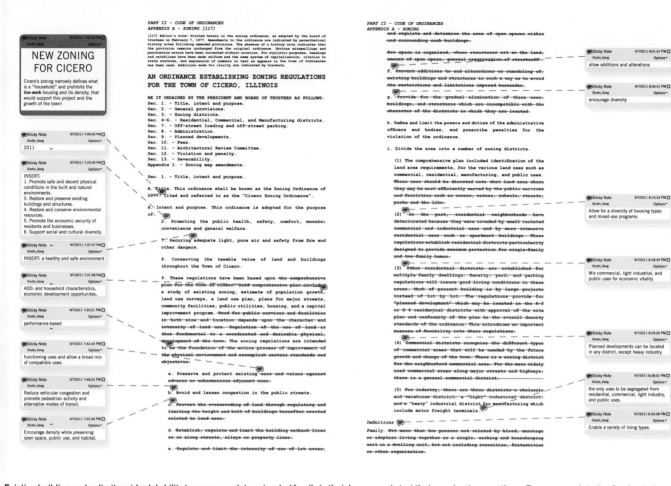

Existing building codes limit residents' ability to accommodate extended family in their homes and start their own businesses there. To accommodate the Garden in the Machine project, these codes would have to be revised.

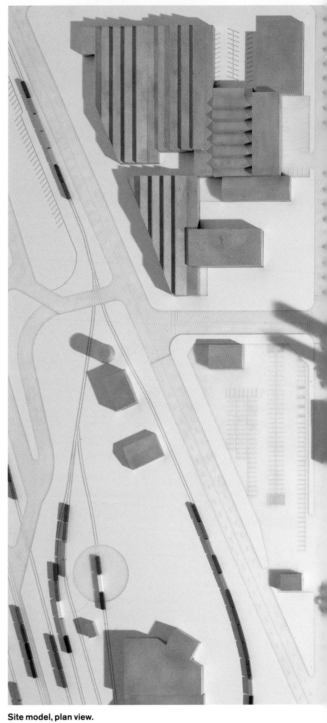

Site model, plan view.

CLOSED HOUSES

THE FORECLOSED FACTORY
OWNERSHIP MODEL

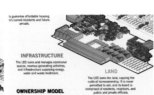

INFRASTRUCTURE
The LEC owns and manages communal
spaces, revenue-generating activities,
and infrastructure supplying energy,
water and waste treatment.

LAND
This LEC owns the land, capping the
costs of homeownership. It is never
permitted to sell, and its board is
comprised of residents, neighbors, and
public and private officials.

OWNERSHIP MODEL

LAND

OWNERSHIP MODEL

FORECLOSED HOU
are purchased from the banks
LEC, joining a cooperative net
established by the Federal Ho
Finance Agency.

LIVE WORK PLAY
Residents own private live-and-work
spaces and pay for services. All shares
are bought and sold through the trust,
guaranteeing stable prices and liquidity.

American Dream
20 C

Coop

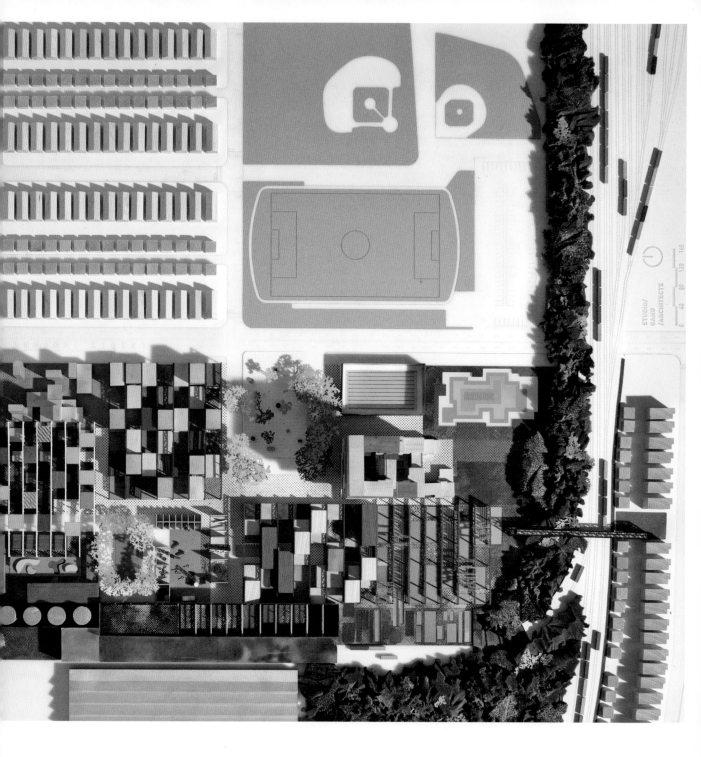

Left, and p. 99: stills from
Zoning and Owning, a
film produced as part of
the project.

Above and right: the Vertical Neighborhood architectural model.

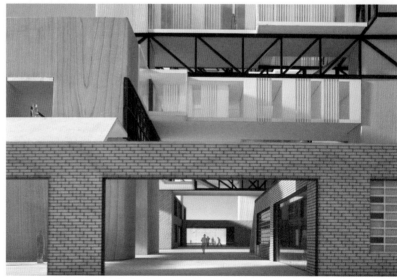

Rendering of the shared courtyard. Residents enjoy access to a variety of gardens and outdoor spaces, including terraces, courtyards, plazas, markets, and allotment gardens.

Rendering of vertical neighborhoods connected by a market and low-rise living and working units.

The nutrient-rich soil of newly cleansed industrial land is used to grow not only trees but food for residents. Functional wetlands treat municipal wastewater. Trees are deployed along rail lines to create regional wildlife corridors.

Questions for the Teams
Jeanne Gang

What aspects of *The Buell Hypothesis* helped you to frame your project? In what ways do you depart from *The Buell Hypothesis*, and why?

Our project addresses the dual crisis of foreclosure and environmental devastation framed in *The Buell Hypothesis*. The environmental imperative for inner-ring suburbs like Cicero, however, centers not on addressing sprawl but on the postindustrial landscape. A long history of lax environmental regulations has created the need to remediate these heavily worked, contaminated lands, and this kind of renewal is an urgent and costly prerequisite for reimagining the inner ring.

We also take up the *Hypothesis*'s issues of ownership patterns and the balance between public and private interests. In our project we propose the creation of a Limited Equity Cooperative that would decouple the live-and-work units from the land on which they sit. Through this system, residents are able to purchase and sell shares corresponding to the units they occupy, without coming to own the land and the shared amenities of the community. This form of ownership strives to guarantee affordable housing to Cicero's current residents and future arrivals.

We depart from the *Hypothesis* in its definition of the American Dream as a ubiquitous notion that includes ownership of home and land. Our research told us that first- and second-generation immigrants have a different dream: that of opportunity for themselves and their children. In order to create this kind of opportunity, our project focused as much on redesigning public policy and financial systems as on designing new infrastructure for a transformed type of home ownership. Buell focuses on redreaming the American city by way of the American house/home. The Garden in the Machine reimagines American arrival and jobs in order to create a new vision of the home and the city.

How would you describe the interaction of housing, infrastructure, and urbanism in your project?

Our site, a defunct factory shell surrounded by blocks of bungalows and sports fields, represents the former practice (and policy) of separating places of work, dwelling, and recreation into distinct "monocultures." Our project demonstrates how these activities can be interwoven to create exciting variety and increased opportunities for residents. Salvaged trusses from the mammoth factory are reused to build smaller work spaces with dwellings above, below, and adjacent to them. The units can be joined, added to, or shared to accommodate the changing employment and household structures of their inhabitants. Communal public amenities, such as a school, market, and car share, are all part of the infrastructure and work to connect the new neighborhood to the existing fabric of Cicero.

How does this project depart from your practice to date? How did you interact with the nondesigner members of your team? What additional expertise do you now wish you might have had as integral to your work, if any?

Our practice is a highly collaborative one that engages multidisciplinary teams on a regular basis. This project, however, cut across a greater variety of issues than we typically address, and led me to reach out to a unique set of participants. Roberta Feldman and Rafi Segal contributed their deep experience in public housing and urban design respectively. Kate Orff contributed her perspective on former industrial sites and regional landscape systems. Through working as an artist in Cicero's neighborhoods, Theaster Gates gained a close understanding of what was important to the town's residents, while Greg Lindsay, an insightful journalist and urban observer, was able to bring cohesion to many of the larger global and financial issues that our project addresses.

What aspects of your project are specific to your site or suburban municipality? What aspects could be extended to other sites across the country?

Cicero's predominant housing stock is composed of brick bungalows, built in the 1920s, that are organized into residential blocks. Its fabric is relatively compact compared to postwar suburbs. Also specific to Cicero is its ethnic demographic: 88 percent of the residents are Hispanic, many of them either immigrants or children of immigrants originating from one of three states in Mexico. Cicero's diverse household structures include extended families, related families, growing families, and even unrelated workers.

Although these figures are specific to Cicero, its "arrival city" characteristics are shared by many other places in the United States and around the world The need that our design addresses—to accommodate the changing circumstances of residents many of whom are immigrants—is a national and global one. In addition, our strategy of interweaving zoning, Limited Equity Cooperatives, and remediated and reused factories could be applied to other sites across the country. Given today's rising rates of unemployment, poverty, and environmental degradation, this kind of comprehensive solution is in fact a necessity.

How might you use this workshop as a teaching tool?

Many members of our project team teach, and I can see ideas about the suburbs, housing, and the many related issues that we explored in the workshops filtering out through them and myself as studio topics. There will also be opportunities to share this work and research with municipalities that face similar issues, as well as—most important—with the people of Cicero itself.

KEIZER
ORE.

0   1.25   2.5 mi.

Nature-City project

- - - -   Keizer municipal boundary
░░░░   Publicly supported development sites
▨▨▨   Nature-City area of influence

The key characteristics of Keizer, Oregon, the site selected in the Pacific Northwest, include a significant poverty rate, a relatively diverse racial makeup, and an active climate for local economic development and planning, with several opportunities for intervention being publicly supported. Keizer was also chosen for its relationship to nearby Salem.[1] In every other *Buell Hypothesis* case study, the city that forms the hub for our representative suburb has been fairly well defined. The population of Salem, though—around 150,000—is relatively small compared to the other city centers we've looked at, making it less clear whether Keizer is a suburb of Salem or whether the combined Salem-Keizer area is a regional suburb of Portland. Either way, with the introduction of a proposed high-speed rail line and the improved transportation this will bring, Salem and Keizer are poised to benefit from new employment opportunities.

One final reason for selecting Keizer (one that is also unique among the examples in the workshop) is that real estate development in the region is limited by the urban growth boundaries set by the state of Oregon. Defined for every metropolitan area in the state, these boundaries are approved by Oregon's Land Conservation and Development Commission in accordance with the Statewide Planning Goals and Guidelines. Generally speaking, urban growth boundaries are intended to preserve greenbelts and agricultural lands and to encourage infill and densification in urban cores.

Local Economy

The economies of Keizer and Salem are intertwined, especially given their joined development restrictions. During the 1990s the area sought to diversify its economic base by attracting technology manufacturing, with limited success. Salem is home to the Oregon State Penitentiary and the state's Department of Corrections headquarters, which largely accounts for the fact that 24 and 20 percent of Keizer's and Salem's working population, respectively, are employed in government jobs. As development is confined within the urban growth boundary, so too are the foreclosures in Salem and Keizer. Given that the area's population is smaller than in our other suburbs, the February 2009 foreclosure rate (fig. 1) is on par with theirs, with the exception of Rialto, which is an extreme case.

Local Conditions

Salem-Keizer's residential rental rate is surprisingly high (fig. 2). The national average for renter-occupied housing is 33 percent: in Salem-Keizer, most of the occupied housing units are rented, with large areas containing upward of 60 percent renters. Although the percentage of renters in Keizer is lower than in Salem, its rate is still higher than the national average and much higher than that of most suburbs.

Fig. 1

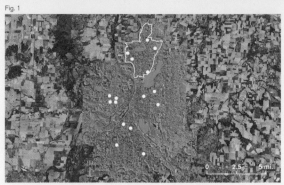

Properties foreclosed on during February 2009
Publicly supported development sites

Fig. 2

Housing units that are rented

0 30 40 50 60%

Fig. 3

Population over 64

0 10 20 30 40%

Fig. 4

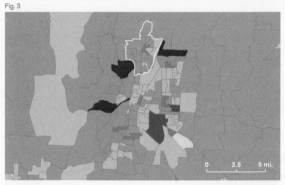

Population over 25 without a high school diploma

0 5 10 15 20%

An important population demographic here is the percentage of the population over the age of sixty-four (fig. 3). Most of the suburbs in the study fit within national trends, and the trend for this particular demographic in the United States is toward slightly less than 13 percent of the population. In most of Keizer and Salem, however, the over-sixty-four population is more than 20 percent, and in several areas it reaches as high as 30 and 40 percent.

In most of the area, the adult population lacking a high school diploma is above the national average of 15 percent. In fact, more than 20 percent of the population has not earned that degree (fig. 4). Along with the continuing talk of suburban growth, transit-oriented development, and economic recovery, Salem-Keizer needs discussion of investment in social infrastructures, notably education.

Local Planning

To the chagrin of many local residents, a long-standing ban on big-box retail stores in Keizer was recently lifted as part of planning strategies aimed at economic development. In response, a group called "Keep Keizer Livable" has sought to preserve the area's small-town, smaller-scale character. In addition to this initiative, there are four designated "urban renewal areas" in Keizer and Salem, and plans for new residential zones. Active planning in both Keizer and Salem has designated over 2,000 combined acres within the urban growth boundary for redevelopment or renewal, with almost $100 million allocated by separate agencies in each city for these areas. With necessarily integrated strategies, the agencies involved in land use and redevelopment include Keizer's Planning Commission and Urban Renewal Agency and Salem's Urban Development Department, Urban Renewal Agency, and Housing Authority. In addition to these agencies, both cities have a variety of commissions, committees, and advisory boards dedicated to specific projects or developments. These include Keizer's Bikeways Committee and individual entities for Keizer's River Roads Renaissance project and Salem's separate urban renewal areas. The existing plans have all proposed combining housing and economic development, with many individual projects intended specifically to stabilize and eventually improve property values.[2]

Possible Sites

Many of the publicly identified redevelopment sites in the area are located in the Keizer Station Urban Renewal Area, the Salem North Gateway Urban Renewal Area, and the West Salem Residential Zone. In many cases, plans have included environmental remediation and public infrastructural improvement designed to attract private investment.

1. Sources: Oregon Department of Land Conservation and Development, "Goals," http://www.oregon.gov/LCD/goals.shtml. U.S. Census Bureau Fact Sheet, "Keizer city, Oregon: 2005–2009 American Community Survey 5-Year Estimates," http://factfinder.census.gov/servlet/ACSSAFFFacts?_event=Search&geo_id=&_geoContext=&_street=&_county=keizer&_cityTown=keizer&_state=04000US41&_zip=&_lang=en&_sse=on&pctxt=fph&pgsl=010. U.S. Census Bureau Fact Sheet, "Salem city, Oregon: 2005–2009 American Community Survey 5-Year Estimates," http://factfinder.census.gov/servlet/ACSSAFFFacts?_event=Search&geo_id=&_geoContext=&_street=&_county=salem&_cityTown=salem&_state=04000US41&_zip=&_lang=en&_sse=on&pctxt=fph&pgsl=010.

2. City of Keizer Department of Community Development, "Keizer Station Plan," April 2007, http://www.keizer.org/commdev/KS/keizer%20station%20plan.pdf. City of Salem Urban Development Department, "North Gateway Urban Renewal Plan (corrected June 2009)," June 2009, http://www.cityofsalem.net/Departments/UrbanDevelopment/UrbanRenewalAreas/Documents/ng_urp.pdf. City of Salem Urban Development Department, "West Salem Urban Renewal Plan (corrected August 2009)," August 2009, http://www.cityofsalem.net/Departments/UrbanDevelopment/UrbanRenewalAreas/Documents/ws_urplan.pdf.

Rendering of WORKac's Nature-City project for Keizer, Oregon. All visual materials in this section produced by WORKac.

WORKac
NATURE-CITY

Ebenezer Howard
Urban Growth Boundaries

The team headed by Amale Andraos and Dan Wood of WORKac asked a simple but challenging question about suburbia: "What if we could live sustainably *and* close to nature?" Reinventing the "Town-Country"—the classic term for the garden city, coined in 1899 by the British urbanist Ebenezer Howard—as a twenty-first-century "Nature-City," the project integrates density, diversity, mixed use, and a variety of housing types across a wide range of affordability with publicly accessible nature, ecological infrastructure, sky gardens, urban farms, and large swaths of restored native habitats.

Cities in Oregon are required by law to establish an urban growth boundary (UGB) to protect open land outside city borders, encouraging densification within existing boundaries and holding otherwise highly desirable forest or farmland as rural amenities. In the case of Keizer, a suburb of Portland that lies on a possible high-speed rail connection between Eugene, Oregon, and Seattle, Washington, a survey of developable lands within the boundary included a 225-acre site at the north edge of town, a site identified for sale. In 2009–10, twenty-eight acres of this site sold for $28 million to be developed commercially with a series of big-box stores, adjacent to an older residential quarter of modest single-family houses, as a first phase of a planned retail development of the entire site. In addition, Keizer expects a population increase of some 13,000 people in the next two decades and is currently debating whether to expand the UGB.

WORKac rolled the clock back to 2009 and designed an alternative scenario to accommodate all of the planned growth on the 225 acres. Their model brings both higher density and more sustainable living to the metropolitan edge, where the greatest development pressures have long existed across the country, while at the same time providing larger economic growth for the city and the site. This radical new vision of suburban living combines the density generally associated with large cities with a direct connection to nature, not only as vista but as recreation and as a mechanism for ecological infrastructure.

Several of the existing streets of the town's residential grid are extended toward the UGB in a series of urban "piers," creating new types of housing and suburban blocks. Between these piers, newly planted woods create a dense natural setting, from an oak savannah to wetlands and a Douglas fir forest. The project includes an impressive variety of housing types, ranging from partywall town houses along the edges to multiunit housing in various forms, from towers with hanging gardens and interior cascades to courtyards, serpentine-shaped buildings and other arrangements of apartment units— all oriented to have unlimited views as well as immediate access to the nature around and in between them. The project provides a set of eye-catching structures, set in greenery, along the highway. At the same time, through its specific shapes, each housing type offers vital services for the town as a whole. The rounded, ziggurat-like housing, for instance, which provides terraces and yards as well as wraparound apartments, is built atop a domed plant that processes organic waste into compost. This in turn creates methane gas, which runs a fuel cell in another block to provide electricity for the whole community. The swimming pool above the complex is warmed by excess heat from this plant. Both the serpentine-shaped and the courtyard housing provide playgrounds, parks, and even aquaponic fishing ponds, as well as blackberry-bush gardens for public foraging. A whole range of ecological functions makes for a city infrastructure that promotes sustainable living as a shared individual and communal undertaking, at the same time that it generates new living experiences and new kinds of public spaces from its various components. The WORKac team even collaborated with advertising experts to create an ad campaign that could help sell this life-style, which builds on the ethos of harmony with nature already valued in Oregon.

public foraging

As WORKac explains it, the project can be built by developers working in partnership with the town, which would benefit from and provide maintenance for the open spaces through a traditional system of property taxes. The housing would offer diversity, being half rental, half ownership, as well as 30 percent affordablehousing, 70 percent market-rate housing. The units would vary in size from studio to three bedrooms, providing for a diversity of living accommodations and population. The efficiencies of high-density construction, the reduction in roads, and the effects of sustainable infrastructure would keep costs within range of current local housing prices. Maintenance would be much reduced, even taking into account public management of all the open spaces. The amount of hardscape would be reduced radically from the typical suburb, making for both less runoff in Oregon's rainy weather and fewer roads to build and maintain. While this new area of Keizer would be five times denser than the adjacent suburban blocks, it would also have three times the amount of open space, all of it public, including a 158-acre natural preserve of native ecosystems. Commercial office and retail spaces would be intermixed and combined with public transportation, making a pedestrian life-style easy. As WORKac put it, "You can live, work, can food, rock-climb, and walk to the movies all in the same day. You can live in a tower of houses or on a hilly rooftop pond."

5x more dense
3x more open space

Above and p. 113: Keizer, Oregon. 2011.

Diagrams showing WORKac's analyses of, clockwise from top left, public transportation, animal habitats, infrastructure, and shared landscapes in the area.

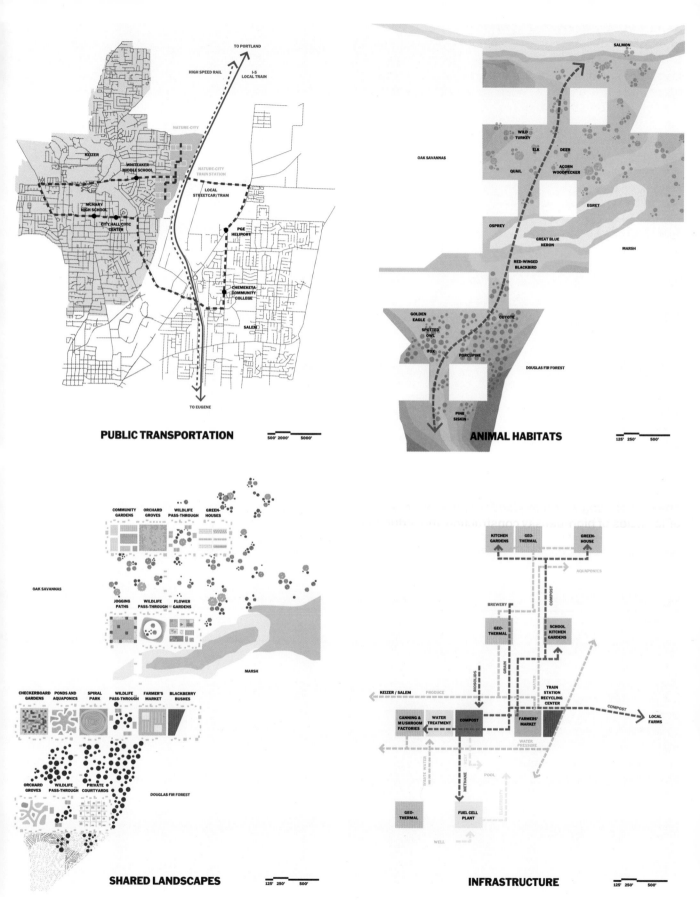

PUBLIC TRANSPORTATION

500' 2000' 5000'

ANIMAL HABITATS

125' 250' 500'

SHARED LANDSCAPES

125' 250' 500'

INFRASTRUCTURE

125' 250' 500'

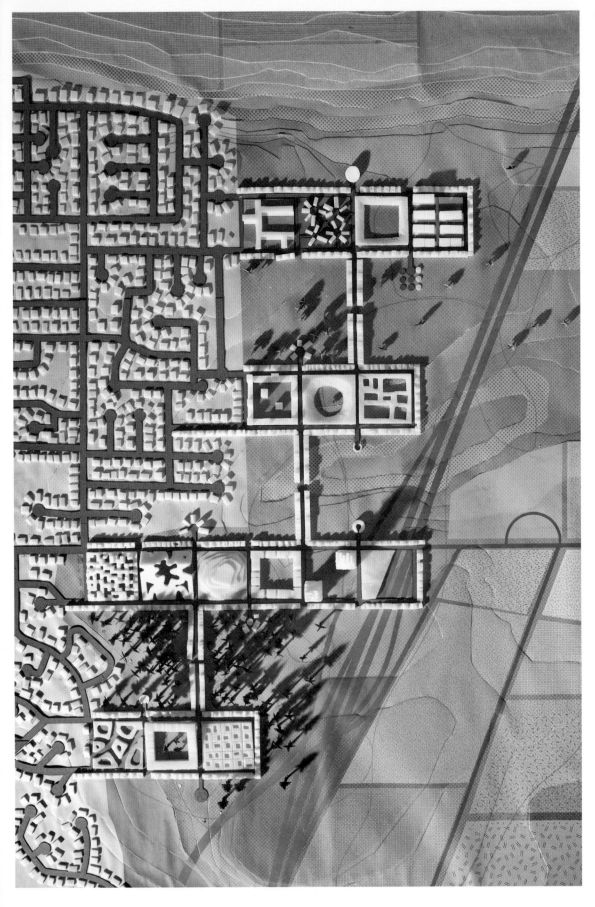

COMPOST HILL

TERRACED HOUSING
+
METHANE DOME
+
SPIRAL PARK

THRU-DE-SAC

CUL-DE-SAC COURTYARDS
+
GEOTHERMAL
+
FORAGING GARDENS

TOWER OF HOUSES

STACKED LIVE-WORK "HOUSES"
+
WATER PRESSURE WATERFALL
+
FARMER'S MARKET

FIELD HOUSES

BROWNSTONES
+
GEOTHERMAL
+
COMMUNITY GARDENS

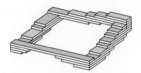

ANGLE

STEPPED SLABS
+
WILDLIFE PASS-THROUGH
+
ROOFTOP LANDSCAPES

HOUSING BRIDGE

PARTY-WALL, MULTI-FAMILY HOUSES
+
LANDSCAPE BRIDGE
+
CARVED COURTYARDS

PIXEL

STAGGERED TOWNHOUSES
+
MUSHROOM & CANNING FACTORIES
+
CHECKERBOARD GARDENS

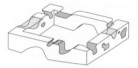

CAVERNS

SLABS
+
WILDLIFE PASS-THROUGH
+
LANDSCAPED CAVERNS

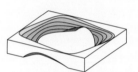

STADIUM

ARENA HOUSING
+
WILDLIFE PASS-THROUGH
+
JOGGING PATHS

HUTONGS

PATIO HOUSING
+
FUEL CELL / POWER PLANT
+
PRIVATE COURTYARDS

SOLAR COURTYARDS

INNER COURTS
+
PUBLIC SCHOOL
+
FLOWER GARDENS

LOWRISE OF HOMES

PARTY-WALL, MULTI-FAMILY HOUSES
+
LANDSCAPE EDGE
+
CARVED COURTYARDS

WATER GARDENS

HILL HOUSES
+
NATURAL WATER TREATMENT
+
PONDS AND AQUAPONICS

POTATO ROWS

ROW HOUSES
+
ROOFTOP GREENHOUSES
+
WINTER GARDEN

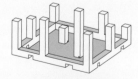

TOWER CLUSTER

STACKED INDIVIDUAL APTS
+
GEOTHERMAL
+
SPORTS FIELDS

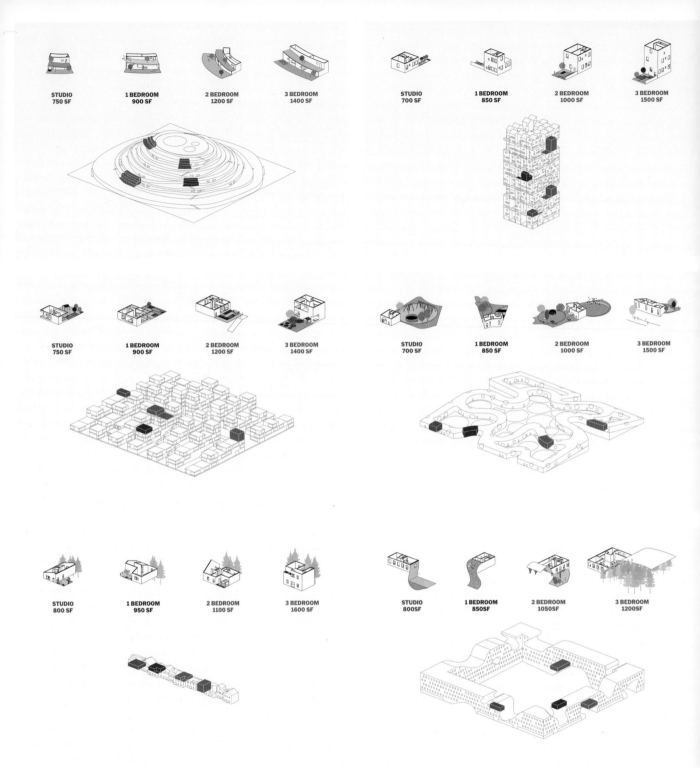

STUDIO
750 SF

1 BEDROOM
900 SF

2 BEDROOM
1200 SF

3 BEDROOM
1400 SF

STUDIO
700 SF

1 BEDROOM
850 SF

2 BEDROOM
1000 SF

3 BEDROOM
1500 SF

STUDIO
750 SF

1 BEDROOM
900 SF

2 BEDROOM
1200 SF

3 BEDROOM
1400 SF

STUDIO
700 SF

1 BEDROOM
850 SF

2 BEDROOM
1000 SF

3 BEDROOM
1500 SF

STUDIO
800 SF

1 BEDROOM
950 SF

2 BEDROOM
1100 SF

3 BEDROOM
1600 SF

STUDIO
800SF

1 BEDROOM
850SF

2 BEDROOM
1050SF

3 BEDROOM
1200SF

Unit typologies in the proposal. Clockwise from top left: Compost Hill, Tower of Houses, Water Gardens, Caverns, Lowrise of Homes, and Pixel.

Architectural model, showing the Water Gardens building.

Architectural model, showing the Caverns building.

Rendering of Compost Hill. This building combines terraced housing and a spiraling park with an interior dome that collects methane from solid waste and produces compost. Waste heat warms public pools at the rooftop.

Architectural model, showing the Bridge Houses.

Architectural model, showing the Caverns building with wildlife pass-through and po

Architectural model, showing Compost Hill and the Water Gardens building.

Architectural model, showing the Pixel building.

121   Keizer, Oregon

Rendering of the Caverns (left) and the Tower of Houses. The Caverns combines housing with caves, ponds, and rock-climbing. The Tower of Houses comprises three-story units, with triple-height gardens, that can be used for living, working, or a combination. An interior waterfall provides water pressure for the entire Nature-City.

Architectural model.

Nature-City advertising campaign.

YOUR HOUSE DOESN'T LOOK LIKE EVERY OTHER HOUSE.

BE ROOMMATES WITH NATURE.

WASTE DOESN'T GET WASTED.

WEAN YOURSELF OFF OIL.

FRESH AIR YOU'LL GET USED TO IT.

Questions for the Teams
Amale Andraos and Dan Wood

What aspects of *The Buell Hypothesis* helped you to frame your project? In what ways do you depart from *The Buell Hypothesis*, and why?

We took *The Buell Hypothesis* very seriously as the brief for our project. Statements such as "All housing is public housing," "Housing *is* infrastructure," and "Change the dream, change the city" were extremely influential and helped us to organize our team and focus our efforts throughout the design process.

Where we departed from the *Hypothesis*, perhaps, was in our decision not to make a visible *architectural* difference between affordable or public housing and market-rate housing. In fact we consciously made them identical, and integrated them within the housing framework, proposing a mix within multiunit, multifamily buildings. While we agree and embrace the urge to reconsider public housing, we do not believe that segregated islands of public housing have been successful. Finally, while we did not shy away from architecture and the design of the buildings and units, we embraced urbanism and infrastructure a bit more closely than what was originally anticipated in *The Buell Hypothesis*.

How would you describe the interaction of housing, infrastructure, and urbanism in your project?

Our project is centered on the notion that housing, infrastructure, and public space can all be combined with new housing typologies to create new forms of living:

Urbanism supplies the minimal grid—the frame—that creates a constant urban interior fabric in Nature-City, and establishes the wide swaths of nature in between. The grid creates blocks that are approximately the size of Portland's; they are "intermediate" in scale—small enough to avoid becoming megablocks yet big enough to explore new housing typologies that are integrated with various shared infrastructures. What frames this diversity is the "Lowrise of Homes," which lines the perimeter of the grid and establishes a "generic" housing typology that is common to the entire city.

Infrastructure is seen primarily as new forms of ecological infrastructure that service Nature-City, and to a lesser degree the neighboring town of Keizer to the west and farms to the east. Each of the larger housing typologies is designed to integrate and organize this new infrastructure: the methane dome, for example, gives the "Compost Hill" housing its spiral shape and organization. The public pools on the roof take advantage of excess heat generated from the methane process. (The definition of "infrastructure" is also expanded to include the "pass-through" buildings, which allow wildlife and landscape to pass across the urban "piers" of the site.)

Housing celebrates diversity by creating a myriad of different choices for inhabitants of the city, from towers to terraced housing to townhouses. Each housing type not only contains infrastructure but is also always paired with a different type of public green space, replacing the monotony of the suburban lawn: from water gardens to spelunking courtyards to community gardens. The types of units provided are also diverse, and completely mixed within buildings: 50 percent rental, 50 percent sales; 70 percent market rate, 30 percent affordable; 20 percent studios, 30 percent one-bedrooms, 30 percent two-bedrooms, 20 percent three-bedrooms.

How does this project depart from your practice to date? How did you interact with the nondesigner members of your team? What additional expertise do you now wish you might have had as integral to your work, if any?

For a number of years, our practice has explored the possible relation between urbanism and ecology, as well as between infrastructure and architecture. And while we have explored "fragments" of ideas in various projects, *Foreclosed* was our first opportunity to put all the pieces together and test whether we could create a comprehensive vision out of traditionally opposed entities: Nature/City, Density/Open Space, Architecture/Urbanism, etc. The project brought our past thinking about "utopia" together with very real considerations, a difficult negotiation of MoMA and Keizer as audiences, as well as intense conversations and constructive debates with our experts. It was a unique set of advisors. The presence of Eric Sanderson (advocating for "ecology") and Gerald Frug (advocating for "city" in terms of both urban density and public space) particularly forced us to create a project that simultaneously addressed and catered to these two poles. Sherwood Engineers and HRA Advisors pushed us to incorporate real, workable solutions for the ecological and financial infrastructure and underpinnings of the project. John McMorrough was our in-house architecture critic, and Wieden Kennedy is helping us to seduce the American public into accepting a new dream for the twenty-first century.

What aspects of your project are specific to your site or suburban municipality? What aspects could be extended to other sites across the country?

The project is highly specific in finding the "problem" in Keizer, a problem that became a pretext for the project: namely, the struggle between Keizer and neighboring Salem over the expansion of the urban growth boundary to accommodate the projected population influx. We also chose Keizer for its very clear situation within an urban-rural-ecological transect. Michael Etzel, an architect born and raised in Keizer, joined our team early on and helped to frame some of the issues. As a result, we were able to communicate with the local newspaper, the *Keizer Times*, and to present the project in Keizer as well as in Salem, with a surprisingly open and positive local response.

At the same time, the project is also quite generic, addressing issues of density and ecology found elsewhere. The types of housing and infrastructure are new, but the square blocks could almost be placed anywhere, creating a new kind of grid out of the suburban cul de sacs with a ratio of "five times the density, three times the open space." The scheme was also developed with the idea that it could be adapted to conditions other than the edge of a suburb.

How might you use this workshop as a teaching tool?

How to formulate an argument out of a massive amount of information, how to edit that information and conceptualize the grounds for a project: this is one of the most difficult aspects of teaching, and going through the workshop—being "students" again—will certainly help us to better explain what it means for students to clearly articulate a project. How to seek expertise and create a team of experts/critics to support and help test the overall argument, how to direct discussions, integrate various, often opposing concerns while maintaining an overall architectural intent, both deeply integrated and autonomous: all of these aspects of the workshop will help in our teaching.

RIALTO
CALIF.

0   1.25   2.5 mi.

Property with Properties project

- - - - Rialto municipal boundary
Publicly supported development sites
Property with Properties area of influence

In early 2008, California Senator Barbara Boxer noted, "The foreclosure crisis is having a dramatic impact across the country. California, which saw some of the greatest increases in housing prices in recent years, is at the center."[1] Rialto, in San Bernardino County, is representative of California in this respect. It also appears in the study as a high-impact area because of its economic conditions (its income and poverty levels) and because of population and housing demographics such as racial and ethnic diversity, housing affordability, and means of transportation for commuters relative to the rest of the region. In the long term Rialto is growing. In fact, because of its position within the Southern California megaregion, its population is expected to increase considerably faster than the national average, gaining 10 percent over five years.[2]

Local Economy

The local economy is largely reliant on the region's transportation networks. Located at the intersection of rail lines heading east from the Port of Los Angeles and highways leading north through California and east to other regions, Rialto is home to regional distribution centers for several corporations. Production, transportation, and material-moving operations currently employ 23 percent of Rialto's civilian workforce.

Fig. 1 does not represent all of the foreclosed properties in Rialto, only those transferred to bank ownership in February 2009. All but a handful of these properties are single-family homes, foreclosed upon by banks that received "bail-out" money from the government's Troubled Asset Relief Program (TARP).

Local Conditions

In Rialto in 2009, 14 percent of the population lived below the poverty line.[3] As is often the case, the distribution of poverty varies: generally, Rialto shows a gradient from a more affluent area in the northwest to increased poverty toward the south (fig. 2). The relatively affluent northwestern corner is made up almost entirely of the sort of single-family housing brought to mind by the term "suburbia" (fig. 3). The percentage of homeowners carrying more than one mortgage on their houses, however, offers another level of insight, involving a household's relationship to homeownership as an investment (fig. 4). If the first mortgage represents what is borrowed to invest in a house, the second mortgage (and/or home equity credit line) represents further credit to which the initial investment provides access. American homeowners often accumulate mortgage debt in order to possess the collateral needed to borrow more. In Rialto, it is largely in those areas with the least poverty and greatest percentage of single-family houses that residents rely most on their houses for access to credit.

Fig. 1

○ Properties foreclosed on during February 2009
■ Publicly supported development sites

Fig. 2

Population living in poverty

0   5   10   15   20%

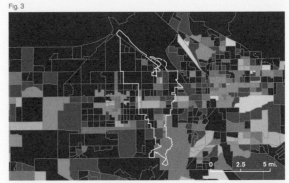

Fig. 3

Housing units that are single-family detached homes

0   5   10   15   20%

Fig. 4

Homeowners carrying more than one mortgage

0   20   40   60   80%

Local Planning

Rialto's public planning efforts have been focused on encouraging both large- and small-scale private development projects for housing and commercial uses to meet its projected population growth and to promote economic development and job creation.[4] The two agencies responsible for Rialto's development are the Redevelopment Agency and the Planning Division, the latter located in Rialto's City Hall. The Redevelopment Agency is in charge of the creation and preservation of Rialto's affordable housing stock. In addition to the city's general plan, the Planning Division creates and implements "specific plans" to address substantial areas for rezoning and redevelopment by private developers.

Possible Sites

Fig. 1 and p. 127 show the areas of Rialto planned by the municipality for private development. As of February 2009, much of this land was publicly owned. Ownership was to be transferred to private developers to realize the city's goals. Among the sites are the 2,400 acres of unincorporated land known as Lytle Creek Ranch, as well as the city's decommissioned municipal airport, renamed Renaissance Rialto.

1. "The Foreclosure Crisis and California: A report by the staff of U.S. Senator Barbara Boxer," January 11, 2008, http://boxer.senate.gov/en/issues-legislation/issues/upload/Senator-Boxer-s-Foreclosure-Crisis-Report.pdf.
2. Sources: ESRI Business Analyst Online, "Market Profile: Rialto RDA," All American Self Storage, "Market Profile: Rialto RDA," http://www.montanaselfstorageunits.com/pdf/rialto-market-profile.pdf. U.S. Census Bureau Fact Sheet, "Rialto city, California: 2005–2009 American Community Survey 5-Year Estimates," http://factfinder.census.gov/servlet/ACSSAFFFacts?_event=Search&geo_id=&_geoContext=&_street=&_county=Rialto&_cityTown=Rialto&_state=04000US06&_zip=&_lang=en&_sse=on&pctxt=fph&pgsl=010.
3. The "poverty line" is an income threshold set annually by the U.S. Census Bureau. It differs according to household size and age of householder. Tables of annual poverty thresholds are available at U.S. Census Bureau, "Poverty," http://www.census.gov/hhes/www/poverty/data/threshld/index.html.
4. City of Rialto Planning Division, "Renaissance Specific Plan," http://www.ci.rialto.ca.us/development_4604.php. City of Rialto Planning Division, "Lytle Creek Ranch Specific Plan," http://www.ci.rialto.ca.us/development_4592.php. City of Rialto Planning Division, "Foothill Boulevard Specific Plan," http://www.ci.rialto.ca.us/development_4650.php. City of Rialto Department of Development Services, "Planning," http://www.ci.rialto.ca.us/development_856.php. Redevelopment Agency of the City of Rialto, "Development Opportunities," http://www.ci.rialto.ca.us/redevelopment_800.php.

Still from *View of Life in the New Development*, an animation produced as part of Zago Architecture's Property with Properties project. All visual materials in this section produced by Zago Architecture.

ZAGO ARCHI-
TECTURE

PROPERTY
WITH
PROPERTIES

Rialto, California. 2011.

Rialto, California, has a long history as a nodal point in Southern California's "Inland Empire"—once a heartland of agribusiness and today one of the largest metropolitan regions in the country, both on its own and as part of the developed fabric that spreads with few interruptions from Los Angeles to Las Vegas. Yet the site chosen here—just outside the current city limits—is the youngest of all the five sites studied in *Foreclosed*. Rosena Ranch is a large residential subdivision, under planning and construction since 2004. Since the financial downturn of 2008, however, work has ground nearly to a standstill, leaving an unexpected juxtaposition: at one end of the site, which is only 10 percent built, nearly identical large-scale houses stand cheek by jowl; at the other end, acres and acres of terraced but unbuilt lots run along broad curving roads, with little vegetation but commanding views of the nearby San Bernardino Mountains. Following a pattern of California development, this unincorporated subdivision would be joined to Rialto upon completion, but today the large grounds of an abandoned airport cut it off from the depressed downtown of the town (whose motto, incidentally, is "Bridge to Progress"), centered around its train station and city hall six miles south. To the north, meanwhile, the I-15 highway separates Rosena Ranch from the beauty of the San Bernardino National Forest. Easily reached from a highway interchange, Rosena Ranch is the absolute prototype of the bedroom suburb, even if Los Angeles is a sixty-minute drive under the best of non-rush-hour conditions.

The Property with Properties proposal is based on the notion that suburbs are, as Andrew Zago, says "ok": "They have their problems, particularly today, but a proposal for a viable future lies in understanding the attraction of their social, economic, and spatial arrangements and creating a new form of architecture and suburbanism from that." Rather than call out the bulldozers and land-contouring equipment to fundamentally remake the unbuilt sector of this failed subdivision, Zago's team—which included an economist, a metropolitan researcher, a land-use specialist, and a landscape architect from the Yale School of Forestry & Environmental Studies—set out to "relax the boundaries" of suburbs as found, creating a richer mix of uses, housing types, living situations, and landscapes than the serial repetition of an individual home with a driveway and a patch of lawn, along overscaled streets that approach metropolitan widths even within view of wide-open nature. Working with the metaphor of "misregistration"—a term referring to a printing-process error that leads to blurred images—Zago developed a system of formally manipulating both housing types and property divisions so that they play themselves out in a series of variations, producing unexpected diversity from a landscape known for sameness. The form of the developer house thus begins to produce configurations shifting from free-standing single-family houses to duplexes and even row houses, creating novel ways of achieving the classic suburban goal of merging indoors and outdoors. At the same time, the planning of the larger site is changed by narrowing the roads and making them more circuitous (without, however, introducing any of the developer suburb's ubiquitous cul-de-sacs), and by overlaying paths for pedestrian movement across the site. Rather than defy the natural characteristics of the site, the proposal allows for both seasonal rivers and wildlife to move in and through it in natural channels, so that the suburb cohabits with the splendor of the adjacent mountains rather than crafting itself as a pastoral place apart. As the new forms produced by misregistration create a great deal of visual variety in the site, they also produce a whole range of possibilities for new mixtures of living, retail, and amenities—in short, as the Zago team describes it, for "a suburb with a richly patterned environment and life-style.... We are giving the property more properties."

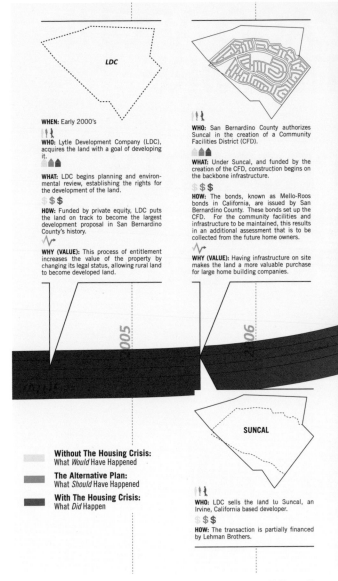

LDC

WHEN: Early 2000's

WHO: Lytle Development Company (LDC), acquires the land with a goal of developing it.

WHAT: LDC begins planning and environmental review, establishing the rights for the development of the land.

$ $ $

HOW: Funded by private equity, LDC puts the land on track to become the largest development proposal in San Bernardino County's history.

WHY (VALUE): This process of entitlement increases the value of the property by changing its legal status, allowing rural land to become developed land.

WHO: San Bernardino County authorizes Suncal in the creation of a Community Facilities District (CFD).

WHAT: Under Suncal, and funded by the creation of the CFD, construction begins on the backbone infrastructure.

$ $ $

HOW: The bonds, known as Mello-Roos bonds in California, are issued by San Bernardino County. These bonds set up the CFD. For the community facilities and infrastructure to be maintained, this results in an additional assessment that is to be collected from the future home owners.

WHY (VALUE): Having infrastructure on site makes the land a more valuable purchase for large home building companies.

Without The Housing Crisis:
What *Would* Have Happened

The Alternative Plan:
What *Should* Have Happened

With The Housing Crisis:
What *Did* Happen

SUNCAL

WHO: LDC sells the land to Suncal, an Irvine, California based developer.

$ $

HOW: The transaction is partially financed by Lehman Brothers.

Diagram of the economic and development model for Property with Properties.

Above, right, and p 134: panoramic images of Rialto, California. 2011.

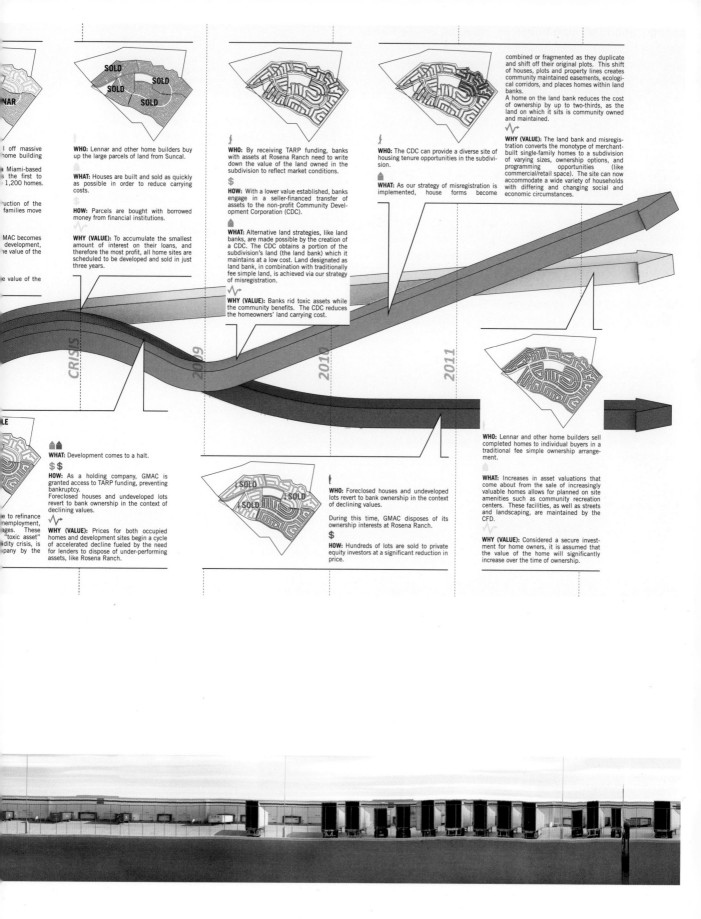

WHO: Lennar and other home builders buy up the large parcels of land from Suncal.

WHAT: Houses are built and sold as quickly as possible in order to reduce carrying costs.

HOW: Parcels are bought with borrowed money from financial institutions.

WHY (VALUE): To accumulate the smallest amount of interest on their loans, and therefore the most profit, all home sites are scheduled to be developed and sold in just three years.

WHO: By receiving TARP funding, banks with assets at Rosena Ranch need to write down the value of the land owned in the subdivision to reflect market conditions.

HOW: With a lower value established, banks engage in a seller-financed transfer of assets to the non-profit Community Development Corporation (CDC).

WHAT: Alternative land strategies, like land banks, are made possible by the creation of a CDC. The CDC obtains a portion of the subdivision's land (the land bank) which it maintains at a low cost. Land designated as land bank, in combination with traditionally fee simple land, is achieved via our strategy of misregistration.

WHY (VALUE): Banks rid toxic assets while the community benefits. The CDC reduces the homeowners' land carrying cost.

WHO: The CDC can provide a diverse site of housing tenure opportunities in the subdivision.

WHAT: As our strategy of misregistration is implemented, house forms become combined or fragmented as they duplicate and shift off their original plots. This shift of houses, plots and property lines creates community maintained easements, ecological corridors, and places homes within land banks.

A home on the land bank reduces the cost of ownership by up to two-thirds, as the land on which it sits is community owned and maintained.

WHY (VALUE): The land bank and misregistration converts the monotype of merchant-built single-family homes to a subdivision of varying sizes, ownership options, and programming opportunities (like commercial/retail space). The site can now accommodate a wide variety of households with differing and changing social and economic circumstances.

WHAT: Development comes to a halt.

HOW: As a holding company, GMAC is granted access to TARP funding, preventing bankruptcy.
Foreclosed houses and undeveloped lots revert to bank ownership in the context of declining values.

WHY (VALUE): Prices for both occupied homes and development sites begin a cycle of accelerated decline fueled by the need for lenders to dispose of under-performing assets, like Rosena Ranch.

WHO: Foreclosed houses and undeveloped lots revert to bank ownership in the context of declining values.

During this time, GMAC disposes of its ownership interests at Rosena Ranch.

HOW: Hundreds of lots are sold to private equity investors at a significant reduction in price.

WHO: Lennar and other home builders sell completed homes to individual buyers in a traditional fee simple ownership arrangement.

WHAT: Increases in asset valuations that come about from the sale of increasingly valuable homes allows for planned on site amenities such as community recreation centers. These facilities, as well as streets and landscaping, are maintained by the CFD.

WHY (VALUE): Considered a secure investment for home owners, it is assumed that the value of the home will significantly increase over the time of ownership.

Labels on image: Outside/Wild, Inside/Garden, Building, Landscape, Mine, Yours, Private/Lawn, Public/Paved

"The Effects of Boundary Relaxation on a Suburban Development," "Before" and "After": the relaxation of demarcations between public and private within the development creates overlaps among previously distinct zones. This mis-registration of boundaries opens a spectrum of new possibilities for home-ownership, landscape defi-nition, building edges, and housing types. Property acquires more properties.

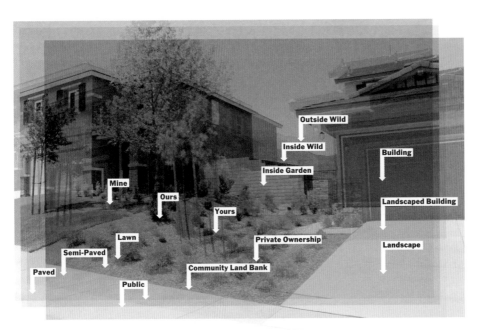

Labels on image: Outside Wild, Inside Wild, Inside Garden, Building, Landscaped Building, Landscape, Mine, Ours, Yours, Private Ownership, Lawn, Semi-Paved, Community Land Bank, Paved, Public

Site plan showing the misregistration of boundaries.

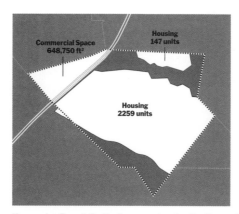
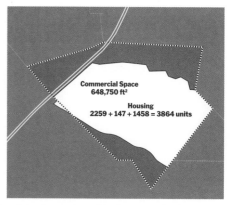

"Increasing Density": site diagrams showing the Rosena Ranch development as originally planned (left) and as proposed by Zago Architecture.

Ownership & Zoning

The relaxation of boundaries (misregistration) within the development creates new categories of land ownership, increasing the paths to home owning and renting and providing mechanisms for maintaining novel circulation and ecological features.

① Private Ownership Zone

In this development the traditional fee-simple model of home ownership remains an option for approximately two-thirds of the homes. Privately owned single-family homes and duplexes in this zone may, in turn, be offered as rental units by the owner.

② Land Bank Zone

A land bank is assembled to provide a lower cost alternative to fee-simple private ownership. The land bank is communally owned and individually maintained. Approximately one-third of the homes are in the land bank zone. Through the land bank, individuals may purchase a home without the land on which it sits. This arrangement greatly reduces the cost of homeownership. Rental units are also made available through the land bank.

③ Maintained

As in traditional subdivisions, streets, infrastructure, and public landscaping are jointly owned and managed by a Community Development Corporation (CDC). Owing to features particular to this development, the CDC also maintains areas of lawn/paving hybrid (grasscrete) and the wildlife corridor.

The Relaxation of Site Boundaries (Misregistration)

Working from the existing layout of streets and lots, misregistration multiplies the meanders and patchwork of the subdivision to create a series of partially overlapping zones. Shown here in color printing's CMYK ink palate are the newly defined areas.

④ Original Subdivision (lawn)

⑤ Original Subdivision (road)

⑥ Site Misregistration 1

⑦ Site Misregistration 2

Site plan, with features and descriptions.

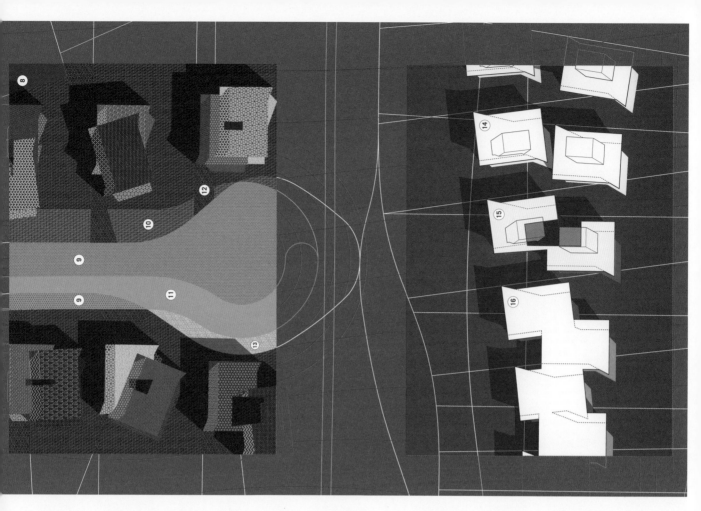

Landscaping & Site Functions

(8) Ecological Zones

In some areas, the misregistration of back property lines opens up large wedges of land along the middle of residential blocks. These areas are used for the project's extensive and varied ecological network. Their proximity to houses encourages a daily interaction with wilderness

(9) Lawn/Paving Hybrids (Grasscrete)

In zones where the misregistration creates an overlap of streets and lawn, a hybrid surface articulation is introduced. Here grasscrete - an open and patterned concrete paving with grass infill - is used. This allows normal traffic to use the narrow paved roads while the grasscrete areas allow for parking, the passage of emergency vehicles and recreation.

(10) Lawn

Large portions of the development allow for suburban lawns or other landscaping of the homeowners' choosing.

(11) Paved Road

These are the existing portions of the original road, greatly reduced in width. The width is based on the "shared surface" model of traffic control in which the presence of pedestrians slows traffic speed.

(12) Driveways & Pedestrian Paths

Side property lines typically divide one lot from the next. In this project they misregister to create driveways and pedestrian paths with overlapping ownership rights.

(13) Stone Paving

Given the overall narrowing of streets, corners and curves are dimensioned more generously with the addition of an alternative paving. Visually distinct from other automotive surfaces and textured to promote slow traffic speed, the alternative paving also illustrates the layering of a misregistration.

Housing Typologies

Misregistration of the site also affects the quantity and layout of homes. It results in a sixty percent net gain of units from 2,406 single-family homes in the original development to a mix of single-family homes, duplexes, and townhouses totaling 3,864 units.

(14) Single-Family Home
2,000 units (52% of subdivision)

The traditional dwelling unit of the suburb accounts for half of all of the units in the new development. These are available as either privately owned, rented, or purchased as a building without land via the land bank CDC.

(15) Attached & Separated Duplexes
1,018 units (26% of subdivision)

In many cases, the original house is duplicated and offset resulting in a rich variety of duplex types. Depending on their configuration and the wishes and needs of the occupants these may be used as either a large single-family house, a shared two-family house, an owner-occupied unit plus a rental unit, or as a residential/commercial hybrid

(16) Townhouses
846 units (22% of subdivision)

Townhouses are created where the offsetting and duplicating of houses results in a continuous string of units.

Modern Home No. 165

1st-Floor Plan   2nd-Floor Plan   3rd-Floor Plan

Four-Bedroom Single Family

This 3-story, 4-bedroom, 2.5-bath house is also available with a carport. It features an open-plan second floor with lanai and a separate exterior staircase. The third floor may be left as an open, loft-like space or enclosed to form a separate home office.

All single-family homes feature:

- Multiple move-in options: available for purchase through either a conventional bank mortgage or from the community land bank and also available as a rental.
- Customizable exterior decorative treatment that also provides sun shading.
- Heating and cooling from a central plant.
- Solid construction using a progressive Structural Insulated Panel system (SIPs). Typical details are illustrated below.

Model Home 1: perspective and plans.

Modern Home No. 438

1st-Floor Plan   2nd-Floor Plan   3rd-Floor Plan

Duplex - Two Full Single-Family Homes

Each unit in this 3-story duplex has 3 bedrooms and 3 baths, a lanai plus a family room adjacent to a shared patio. It is also available with an optional carport. The arrangement of the units allows it to be used as either a shared two-family house or as an owner-occupied building with a rental-income unit.

All duplex units feature:
- Multiple move-in options: available for purchase through either a conventional bank mortgage or from the community land bank.
- Customizable exterior decorative treatment that also provides sun shading.
- Heating and cooling from a central plant.
- Solid construction using a progressive Structural Insulated Panel system (SIPs). Typical details are illustrated below.

Model Home 2: perspective and plans.

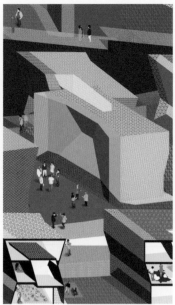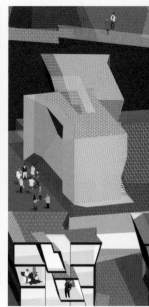

Stills from *View of Life in the New Development.*

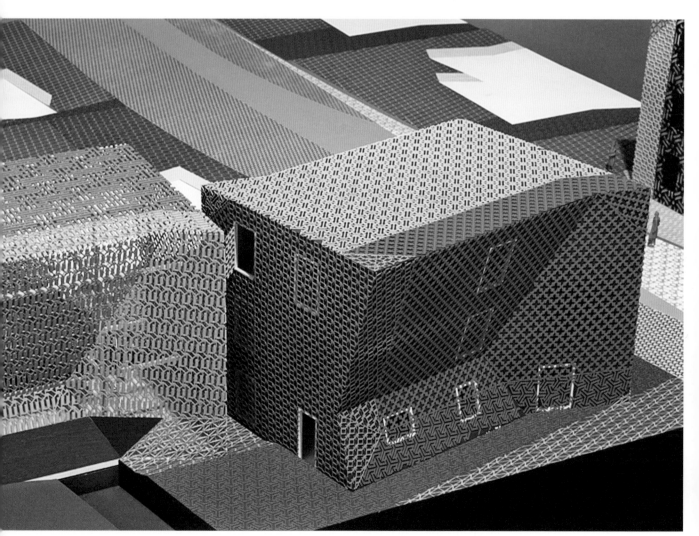

Architectural model showing two single-family homes.

Diagram of circulation within the project.

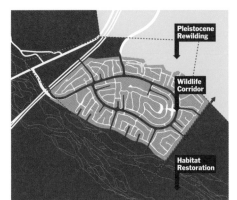

Diagrams of wilderness systems in the project.

Architectural model, plan view.

Questions for the Teams
Andrew Zago

What aspects of *The Buell Hypothesis* helped you to frame your project? In what ways do you depart from *The Buell Hypothesis*, and why?

The Buell Hypothesis frames its topic of study as the American Dream as manifested through the American suburb and single-family homeownership, whose status it considers in light of the foreclosure crisis. Our project embraces these topics. It seeks to redefine the suburban subdivision and the single-family home and to craft alternative means to homeownership in light of this crisis.

The project departs from the goals of *The Buell Hypothesis* in two ways. First, it uses public funding to leverage new forms of ownership (chiefly through the development of a community-held land bank) rather than to provide public housing outright. Second, it views architecture as an open-ended catalyst for new and varied dreams, rather than as a vehicle to instantiate a predetermined dream. In a reversal of a central proposition of the *Hypothesis*, we propose: *Change the city you change the dream.*

How would you describe the interaction of housing, infrastructure, and urbanism in your project?

Spatially, most suburbs are fields defined by networks of infrastructure rather than figures defined by building mass. In the suburban residential subdivision, houses—arrayed along curved streets with hierarchically engineered traffic and utilities—exist as separate and autonomous entities, each on its own plot of land. Our project does not erase this network/field but does substantially alter it. In significantly increasing the intended density of the development, we let building mass begin to define an urban space, but only in places, and through a gradual transition from fieldlike conditions. Conversely, while building mass results in more clearly defined urban space, lines of infrastructure become more diffuse and less hierarchical.

How does this project depart from your practice to date? How did you interact with the nondesigner members of your team? What additional expertise do you now wish you might have had as integral to your work, if any?

While my architectural practice has worked on many projects in suburban settings, we have never worked on the problem of suburbs per se. As a collaborative model, the key to our success was the establishment, early on, of an approach that grew from our disciplinary interests in architecture (the relaxation of boundaries, or *misregistration*). This architectural interest was then expanded to the fields of ecology, real estate, and engineering. We had a relatively small team from other disciplines, consisting of an urban financial planner (David Bergman), an ecologist and landscape architect (Alex Felson), and an engineer (Bruce Danziger). This was an

ideal mix of people and fields of expertise. We all felt that a larger team would have diluted the energy and clarity of the project. Were this to go on as an actual project, a larger team of consultants would, of course, be necessary.

What aspects of your project are specific to your site or suburban municipality? What aspects could be extended to other sites across the country?

We approached the project as a case study of the American suburb in general, with key features gauged to address three other scales in increasing specificity. Our project began with the recognizable (iconic) form and layout of the subdivision, the standard unit of aggregation for the American suburb, and grew a new development from that. As an urban morphology, the project has relevance to nearly any suburban community across the country. But it is also specific to the American Southwest, where the population continues to increase and new developments are placed ever closer to wilderness areas. Our general ecological approach conceives of a new, nonexclusory interface between development and wilderness. The legacy of Proposition 13, the 1978 California ballot initiative that limits local governments' ability to raise property taxes, provides another scale of specificity. Our site is a failing subdivision. Its financial model—and our proposed rescue of it—are engineered through mechanisms particular to California. Lastly, our project is context specific in that its design addresses local ecology, demographics, and transportation networks.

How might you use this workshop as a teaching tool?

I regularly run advanced design studios for the Southern California Institute of Architecture's urban studies program (SCI-Arc Future Initiatives). While I wouldn't adapt this workshop model to my teaching, I do plan to use the experience of it in two ways. As a topic, I feel the problem of the single-family home and the American suburb is a valuable area of continued study. As an approach, I would press further our premise: the missing element in American urbanism is architecture. The pedagogical lesson is that with all the value other disciplines bring to urbanism, new urban projects should be not only architect-led, but *architecture*-led.

Public Property
Reinhold Martin

Fiddling while Rome burns? No. That would be mixing metaphors. Actually, it's Athens. And it's more like crumbling than burning. As the materials from the *Foreclosed* workshop were being prepared for exhibition, the finance ministers of Europe and officials from international banking institutions were contemplating the fiscal fate of Greece, with the thought that Italy could be next. Meanwhile, Wall Street and other representative urban sites across the United States were being "occupied." It may therefore seem myopic to limit a study like this one, which had its origins in the financial crisis of 2008, to the American suburbs. But we live in a world where the brutal and long-planned dismantling of the modern welfare state, whatever its problems may have been, is being authorized by an ongoing crisis linked in part, and through a series of mediating levels, to subprime home-mortgage defaults. In this world, Athens, Greece, and Athens, Georgia, are intimately connected.

That, in any case, is the opening proposition of *The Buell Hypothesis*: that globalization, and the responsibility for its consequences, begin at home. When we say "global" we are not speaking merely of transnational financial institutions swapping algorithms, or of profound but diffuse multiculturalism. We are also speaking of real, material things, like houses. Not "assets," but things in and through which life is lived. So it is by no means myopic to focus on a housing crisis in the American suburbs. On the contrary, it opens a window on the world. But what do we see through this window?

In *The Buell Hypothesis*, drafted as a screenplay, we saw first of all two philosophers, Socrates and Glaucon. Of course these two are not latter-day incarnations of their Greek namesakes. They are merely ciphers meant to indicate, through a simplified version of the Socratic dialogue, that we are dealing here with philosophical matters best suited to exposition in such a manner. Write your own name into one of their roles. If there is a script here, it is for a film yet to be made, a drama—some would say a tragedy, others, a farce—of epic proportions, laid out in genial, conversational prose in the front seat of a car. It is a documentary film about what can and cannot be imagined in the real world, and about what is or is not "common" about common sense.

Public property. In some sense an oxymoron, this was the main "deliverable" of the second, practical section of *The Buell Hypothesis*, which has been absorbed into the documentary material contained in *Foreclosed*. In the original, the scene was an academic symposium presided over by Diotima, a no-nonsense social scientist named after the real Socrates's teacher. One after the other, Diotima's graduate students outline, with data-driven, cartographic precision, the details of eight suburbs across the country. Five of these were selected as sites by the design teams participating in the *Foreclosed* workshop and exhibition. In each case, Diotima's maps also documented a number of large "development sites" owned by the municipality or otherwise in its custody. Implied here was the policy, in the immediate aftermath of the 2008 crisis, of government stepping in to buy out distressed assets, including land, mainly to protect large financial institutions from default. Thus the study was "backdated" to February 2009, which was offered as a fork in the historical road. Like many such moments of truth, that fork revealed a choice that had actually been present all along, and still is. The process of selling public land for real-estate speculation could continue. Or, something else could be done with the land, utilizing public resources, to demonstrate that city-building does not necessarily have to take the path laid out by the markets.

That, in effect, was the choice offered to participants in the *Foreclosed* workshop. Now please don't object that this choice reflects an artificial division of "public" and "private" interests, whereas the "public/private partnerships" actually projected for many of the sites represent a congenial reconciliation of otherwise conflicting interests. On the contrary, philosophically speaking a "public/private partnership" is another oxymoron. In classical Athens, the citizens empowered to debate publicly the virtues of democratic governance were mainly white male property-holders, sovereigns of the *oikos* (or household, the root of both *economy* and *ecology*), inside which labored women and slaves. Hence an abiding and much-commented-upon contradiction, wherein participation in the classical public sphere is secured by private assets.

Our contemporary sense of "public," whether we are referring to discourse or to property, still rests on this contradiction. In the early American republic, for example, no one, not even the framers of the Constitution, could presume that the interests of enslaved persons and the interests of their "owners" could simply be reconciled. Today, some but not all of those conflicts have been mitigated. For if the aftermath of the 2008 crisis demonstrates anything, it is that we still live in a society organized around unresolved antagonisms, rather than partnerships, among different and often opposing interests.

How to confront those differences? Acknowledge them rather than wish them away. Recognize, for example, that there is after all a difference, both practical and philosophical, between "public" housing and "affordable" housing. Articulate that difference, however fragile and contingent it may be, and test its consequences. This was the second challenge posed—gently—to the workshop participants by *The Buell Hypothesis*. In other words, through its dramatis personae, the *Hypothesis* proposes rethinking, let's say remediating, suburban-

ization by developing new, mixed-use but *unapologetically public* housing models on government-owned or -managed land in the municipalities that have been hardest hit by the economic crisis.

Whether the challenge was met or evaded in the workshop, it does not imply that architecture and urbanism can "solve" the problem. It only draws a line in the sand. To begin with, there was no problem to be solved, only a storm to be weathered. But underlying this storm there *was* and *is* a problem, a diffuse but systemic one. So the problem for architecture and urbanism here is to *define* the problem. Pose the question by testing the limits of what is given, beginning with the nature of the "property" on which you build, and of the forms of sovereignty and everyday governance that control it.

That was the charge on the side of the polis, or the city/suburb and its constitution. Then there was the aesthetic side. Architecture, like any art, intervenes in the imagination. It helps to make the current world knowable. It also manipulates form and experience, symbolism and utility, to make fragments of possible worlds visible. By laying out its arguments as a film script, *The Buell Hypothesis* analogizes architecture with cinema. Like cinema, architecture to some extent structures the narratives or scenes through which possible futures come into view or are obscured. This can happen through a kind of a stage set on which a hypothetical world might unfold. Or, it can be done by organizing the elements of that world, juxtaposing them, aligning them, connecting them, separating them, such that they open our eyes and rearrange our expectations.

The architectural challenge was therefore an invitation to rewrite the script. In other words, it was an invitation to change the imaginary movie that plays in our heads when we hear an expression like "the American Dream." As with many Greek tragedies, this movie might simply have been updated by modernizing the sets. But it was also possible that the script itself was flawed. To test that proposition literally, we asked each design team to produce a large-format digital "movie" to be exhibited as a key component of their work.

At another level, architecture is simply architecture, a discipline and an art in its own right, with its own problems and its own possibilities. *The Buell Hypothesis* acknowledges as much when Socrates and Glaucon reflect on the architecture of suburban houses and, in particular, on the question of the front door. In this respect, the "design" of the front door presents an eminently architectural challenge that calls forth a whole host of social, economic, and political concerns. As Socrates notes, the suburban habit of entering the house from within the garage raises the strange question of whether the main door ought to be on the outside of the house in the first place. This in turn raises the question of whether entry should be by automobile or on foot. Which in turn causes us to think about possible means of transportation, leading in turn to questions of proximity, density, walkability, mass transit, and so on. All of this coming out of that little door, wherever it is in each of the models in the exhibition. *The Buell Hypothesis* asked the workshop participants to examine such connections, and to redefine what we mean by "house" and "housing" in the first place. That is where the movies and the models come together, hypothetically at least.

I say "hypothetically" because the Buell research is just that: a hypothesis. The exhibition is its test. But I confess that the brief monologue that ends the dialogue, in which Socrates outlines the four points or scales at which his argument unfolds, from the globe to the city to the house to the door, is a bit of a decoy. Or, in experimental terms, it is the control, the minimum expectation, the status quo ante. Yes, at one level, the hypothesis is, as Socrates says: Change the house and you change the city. But at another level, the hypothesis is: Change is not possible under current conditions. Meaning that, unless we learn to say "public" in public again when it comes to housing, there is little hope of doing anything but repeating versions of the arrangement that generated the crisis in the first place. This is different from saying that more public housing, in the suburbs or anywhere else, is the answer. Instead, it says that the problem itself needs to be reformulated, taking into account all of the fragilities and contingencies written into the term "public," a task with which architecture can help.

So that's the test. Do these models and movies enable a new type of conversation barely anticipated by that between Socrates and Glaucon, where the facts on the ground mapped (in the original Buell document) by Diotima and her students provide a basis for a new definition of the problem and, ultimately, a new hypothesis? Are these artifacts capable of assembling publics around them, groups of interested parties ready to debate their merits and their deficits, to assent or to object, all in the name of formulating a new common sense, within which further possibilities might be tested? Can the architecture of housing, in other words, become public property?

It is a difficult task, to be sure, one worthy of that most storied of venues for the disputation of architectural matters, the modern museum. Yet every institution has its limits. Among which in this case is the notorious challenge faced by all architecture exhibitions, of showing not the thing itself (the building, the city) but representations of it (models, movies). To avoid this dilemma, I invite you to suspend disbelief and imagine that you are not looking at representations of things but rather at things in themselves (*simply* models, *simply* movies). These things can compel thought, and maybe action. And so there is no time like the present to watch them do their work. That work, which is also our work, involves reclaiming the public sphere. To get a sense of the critical conversations that might echo through this sphere, the sort that occur after seeing a challenging film, we can imagine Socrates and Diotima running into one another again, perhaps in an airport....

FADE IN

A GENERIC AIRPORT PASSENGER LOUNGE – EARLY EVENING

SOCRATES
Hey, congratulations on the exhibition at MoMA that was based on your research.

DIOTIMA
Yes. *Foreclosed*, on housing and suburbanization. There were fantastic big models and stunning movies.

SOCRATES
But what did you think?

DIOTIMA
That we have a long way to go.

SOCRATES
How so? I was impressed. I mean, look at the thought behind each of those projects—the complexity of issues that each is balancing, the sheer vision. The one by the firm called MOS, for example. I loved their movie. It reminded me of that filmmaker, the guy who made *Blue Velvet*—

DIOTIMA
David Lynch.

SOCRATES
Yeah, that's it. Slow, steady, and strange. And did you see what they proposed? To build housing in the middle of the streets of Orange, New Jersey! They're right—who needs cars when you have a train station nearby, and enough food and services within walking distance? Anyway, it's healthier.

DIOTIMA
Yes, it is. But did you notice that they are proposing that the streets, rather than being owned by the municipality, would now be owned by a co-op? Odd, at a time when the "street" is being reoccupied in a politically meaningful way, whether in Cairo or by protesters in lower Manhattan. Yes, it could be an inclusive co-op (do these exist?), but the streets would have become private property nonetheless. That's more privatization, not less. Even if the surrounding houses eventually fall away without being replaced, do they really think that property will

suddenly become public? It looks like it could become a strange sort of island, an inadvertent gated community, even. Forget David Lynch. It reminds me of that episode of *The Wire* when the police closed off the streets in one near-vacant Baltimore neighborhood to make a zone with its own laws, including legalized drugs. They called it Hamsterdam, or Amsterdam.

SOCRATES
What's wrong with that? I have the catalogue here. Look at the MOS model. It looks like logs floating down rivers. They say Venice was one of their inspirations, meaning I guess a pedestrian city with canals. But you're right, it could have been Amsterdam. Just add bikes. And these houses—quite picturesque, actually. All the same yet each a little different, with different patterns of identical windows. Some have rooms, others have stairs and services; some are connected together, others are more independent.

MOS's Thoughts on a Walking City project. Architectural model, plan view.

DIOTIMA
It sounds like an Internet-age model of community. We're all unique individuals joined together by Facebook.

SOCRATES
Was that sarcastic?

DIOTIMA
No, not at all. I'm only saying that for many today, this seems like common sense. But common sense is historically constructed, and I recall you saying something about it needing to be changed. I too was quite taken by what I can't help calling the "American beauty" of the MOS movie. But that one didn't end so well for Kevin Spacey's character, did it? There's a slow, steady violence hidden in the languor, in the casual sociability.

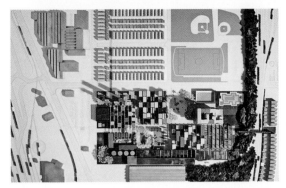

Studio Gang Architects' Garden in the Machine project. Site model, plan view.

SOCRATES
Speaking of violence, I was quite interested in the courageous take on immigration in the Studio Gang project for Cicero, Illinois. Even as guest workers are being hunted down at the southern border, it offers an optimistic vision. Basically, it proposes cultural difference as a means of renewal. It's no accident that this housing for underserved, largely Mexican immigrants is literally built out of the remnants of an old factory.

DIOTIMA
Yes, it's courageous in the sense that it will no doubt be subject to xenophobic derision in certain dark corners of the American "conversation." But the solution is still ownership based, and built on private property. While it's fine for the public sector to incentivize nonprofits to build such things, fundamental issues tend to go unaddressed. As you've said before, the American Dream is ultimately one of homeownership, whether actual or symbolic. Historically, homeownership has also been a key path toward assimilation into the imagined community called the nation for many first- and second-generation immigrants. But is a community composed of property owners the only option?

SOCRATES
So it seems, though ownership here signals flexibility rather than stability. The carnivalesque feel of their movie and the rough-and-ready character of the model suggest improvisation and provisionality.

DIOTIMA
Yes. But that could also be another name for precariousness. And the reanimated industrial ruin has its own precursors in New York's High Line and London's Tate Modern. In such cases our nostalgia for the heroics of the modern city can easily become yet another urban "theme," cleansed of conflicts like those that surely arose in that old Cicero factory when the unions pushed back. Under what conditions can we imagine these workers making political demands, whether as citizens or as

noncitizens? By putting undocumented immigrants on display, the Gang project risks overexposing them. On the other hand, it offers them a site and a platform to claim as their own, insulated from the vicissitudes of the open market.

SOCRATES
Speaking of work, did you see the one with all the trees?

DIOTIMA
You mean the project by WORKac for Keizer, Oregon? Ecologically brilliant, but economically speaking, it's still fundamentally a for-profit project. Why? This remediated land could easily be made public, especially since parks pass through and under it. So why privatize? Here's another conundrum. On the one hand, training the real estate market in "best practices" is crucial. On the other, the predatory character of most development is among the causes of the current economic *and* ecological crises.

WORKac's Nature-City project.
Architectural model, plan view.

SOCRATES
I thought their project did something interesting with the architectural vernacular of the single-family house. Did you see the model? A whole city, or at least a series of block-sized minicities, made up of familiar-looking suburban houses compacted together, and rearranged into dense urban blocks, and even into towers with water filtering through their atriums, and shared lawns made out of methane domes. And wilderness! Even their movie was made in the sophisticated vernacular of advertising,

sort of like a wry TV show, or a commercial that you're not sure is a commercial.

DIOTIMA
Yes. But I'm not sure its reactivated vernacular speaks a different kind of common sense—it's also a kind of western that channels the romance of the "American frontier." I see the cowboys in the model, dressed in business casual. But where are the Indians?

SOCRATES
If I follow your implication, I'd say that it shows us how a developer might build ecologically, integrate a significant amount of less expensive (i.e. "affordable") housing, and still make a profit. The best of all plausible worlds, for many. But it doesn't necessarily show us an alternative to profit-maximizing urban development.

DIOTIMA
There's a pattern here. Innovative financial models, adaptations of market mechanisms like co-ops, land trusts, and even REITs. All designed to cushion the blows, with stunning imagination. But do any offer a structural or systemic alternative?

SOCRATES
OK. But you know, the WORKac project does speak to the middle classes. It's more about Main Street than Wall Street.

DIOTIMA
Sure. But contrary to what they still teach in some architecture schools, Main Street is *not* almost all right. Moreover, what you might imagine to be your local bank, dressed up in neo-Georgian vernacular, is actually "on" Wall Street. So can we really make a new kind of eco-city out of little houses whose mortgages are still held by the local global bank? You can change the house, and even the city, but try changing the bank. That may be harder.

SOCRATES
Touché. Another project that tried to leverage the crisis into an innovative way of regulating development was the Zago Architecture proposal for Rialto, California. The disconnect between its formalism, where the abstracted "house" is hybridized ad infinitum, and the ecological reorganization of the landscape is disorienting. I mean, it sounds so reasonable. But look at it. It's the opposite of vernacular.

DIOTIMA
Yes, it's very stylized. But also very architecturally articulate. Looking at the model, though, I still can't quite figure out what's going on inside the houses. Too bad that it overlooks your point about the car-oriented inside-out

149 Public Property

house. A real missed opportunity for a project devoted to topographic rearrangement. And what is it with the wilderness theme in these projects? Both Zago and WORKac invite wild animals into the yard. It's like the return of a repressed "nature" come back to spread rabies and Lyme disease. Nature as the big Other.

Zago Architecture's Property with Properties project. Architectural model, plan view.

SOCRATES

Well, I don't know. But I do know that Zago's adaptive reuse of a typical suburban subdivision rearranges all sorts of boundaries. Still, like you, I'm tempted to look for those that remain intact despite the blurring and misregistration. Did you see the people in their movie? Live characters inhabiting a patterned, spatially ambiguous background. They don't look much different from the people who might have lived in that subdivision regardless. I'm not sure their minds have changed.

DIOTIMA

Well, you know, Visible Weather's project for Temple Terrace, Florida, does explicitly refuse privatization. It also proposes something close to real public housing. Oddly, they create a commercial entity, a municipally owned Real Estate Investment Trust (REIT) to do so. But they even put City Hall on the second floor of one of the complexes!

SOCRATES

Yes, but what do you make of all those empty chairs in their movie?

DIOTIMA

Well, I get their point about an impossible community under current conditions. At least the project acknowledges the scope of the issue. The model is quite striking but unapproachable. Its base is even rotated on the diagonal to emphasize the corners, like a Renaissance fortress.

SOCRATES

Completely appropriate for a piece of architecture that foregrounds and maybe even aestheticizes the pathos of suburban life. The different apartment types certainly recognize different needs, whereas the different transparencies seem to repel as much as connect.

DIOTIMA

But I fear that, despite its allure, the model gives in too soon, meaning that it shies away from posing the problem in a dialectical fashion. The residents it imagines appear soulless and one-dimensional. Does either the model or the movie give us access to their troubling humanity—not in a sentimental way, but tangibly?

Visible Weather's Simultaneous City project. Architectural model, plan view.

SOCRATES

You mean, in the multiple senses of the term "public"?

DIOTIMA

Yes. Not a falsely universal public of soulful humans, or a public made up of robotic sources of profit, but a multiplicity of thinking publics, assemblies of thoughts and feelings that are neither universal nor attached to any one individual. A problematic, difficult, and constructive multiplicity, always critical, always protesting, always building....

FADE OUT

In closing, there are at least two more points to elicit from the models and movies in the exhibition. First, each of these teams comprised many participants, including students and recent graduates, all of whom made their own contributions. Many of these collaborators would formerly have been called consultants, or experts—planners, economists, landscape designers, ecologists, engineers, community organizers, and so on. Despite the initial emphasis on publicly funded development, many of these collaborations yielded market-based (or at best not-for-profit) innovations. At the same time, few were able to engage directly with the residents of the neighborhoods in which they were designing. Most were understandably wary of uncritical populism; after all, far too many "community design charrettes" are mere public relations contrivances. Still, the relative noninvolvement of actual publics raises the question: How to enter into something like participatory planning, without fetishizing "participation" as an end in itself?

Second, a key element of *The Buell Hypothesis* is its historical dimension. Housing as a matter of public concern was debated vociferously in the press and in the streets throughout the twentieth century in the United States. The urgency of the moment has (again understandably) allowed this long history, recorded in the original document, to slip to one side. But in addition to building new types of cities, architecture can help build historical consciousness. It can remind us that things have not always been this way, and do not need to remain this way. It can also make tangible—and accessible—the complexities involved in bringing about actual, historical change.

You may have heard, perhaps from experts, that certain options are no longer available and must be kept off the table. But more frequently now, we hear informed, historically accurate challenges to such ill-informed "expertise." Without romanticizing past achievements or exaggerating their failures, the work in this catalogue poses such a challenge. It remains to be seen whether we are capable of further transforming our own models and movies, and the dreams we dream about them, into equally transformative realities.

Coda

In one of modernity's most influential extensions of the Western classical tradition, Immanuel Kant famously defined Enlightenment as "mankind's exit from its self-incurred immaturity." Although it would be philosophically reductive to summarize this definition and the imperative it contains simply as "growing up," it would not be entirely inaccurate. Provided, I would add, we recognize that enlightenment, now modestly aware of its unstable place in the world, entails the lifelong, self-critical activity of learning *together*, in this case as architects, urbanists, thinkers, citizens, and cohabitants of a fragile planet.

The essay above, with its fictional dialogue, is intended to encourage further learning. Its occasionally critical tone, conveyed particularly in Diotima's persistent questions, is adopted out of respect for the seriousness and ambition of the works discussed. Throughout the *Foreclosed* project, the Buell Center has sought to act as a pedagogical institution in the broadest sense. When we began the research, we asked: What can we do in a university that would be more difficult to do elsewhere? Our provisional answer was: Learn to say "public" in public again. Hence, we combined science (the science of the city, as recorded in the research and developed by the teams) with philosophy, in the Kantian sense of ongoing critique. So "growing up together" here means learning to extend our critical faculties to take up otherwise foreclosed questions, with the help of scientific instruments made available by our respective fields.

The Museum of Modern Art offered a generous and welcoming laboratory for conducting the ensuing experiment. This laboratory, which is different from that of the university, compels us to evaluate the work—again, together—as a contribution to the culture of architecture and urbanism as well as to society at large. Which, in turn, has challenged the Buell Center to consider further its own role as a cultural institution dedicated to the difficult, modest work of enlightenment. That work would not be possible without the imagination and innovation on display in these pages. We are therefore enormously grateful for the opportunity to work together and very much hope that the conversation, and the work, will continue.

WORK-
SHOPS

A *Foreclosed* orientation, on May 6–7, 2011, at MoMA PS1, included panels and presentations on *The Buell Hypothesis*, the foreclosure crisis, and the work of the five teams. Keynote speakers were Michael Sorkin and Ellen Dunham-Jones. Top row, left: Reinhold Martin; center: Michael Sorkin and Ellen Dunham-Jones; right: one of the panels. Second row, left: Dianne Harris, Robert Beauregard, and Sudhir Venkatesh; center: Robert Beyer in a Q&A session; right: Ellen Dunham-Jones. Third row, left: audience members; center: Jeanne Gang; right: Vishaan Chakrabarti and Robert Beauregard. Fourth row, left: David Smiley; center: Michael Sorkin giving his keynote speech; right: David King and Sarah Gerecke. Bottom row, left: Michael Meredith and Hilary Sample of MOS; center: audience members; right: Robert Beauregard. Other participants, not pictured, included Teddy Cruz, John Goering, Laura Kurgan, Brian Loughlin, Sudir Venkatesh, June Williamson, and project architects.

Back to the Burbs
Michael Sorkin

Michael Sorkin, of Michael Sorkin Studio, New York, and Director of the Graduate Center in Urban Design at The City College of New York, gave this talk at the symposium that kicked off *Foreclosed* on May 7, 2011, at MoMA PS1. Sorkin's references to Socrates and Glaucon refer to the conceit and structure of *The Buell Hypothesis*. Sorkin and Ellen Dunham-Jones, Professor of Architecture and Urban Design at Georgia Tech College of Architecture and a member of the Board of Directors of the Congress for the New Urbanism, were the keynote speakers, tasked to "make sparks fly" and engage in a Socratic debate. Sorkin spoke against the suburb.

I grew up in the suburbs and so address this gathering with a combination of expertise and jaundice. In fact my experience was in many ways pleasant, due in large part to the specific character of the suburb in which I was raised. Located in the then bowery and semi-somnolent climes of Fairfax County, Virginia, the development of my youth—Hollin Hills—was an island of modernity in the rising tide of old colonialoid split-levels. Designed by Charles Goodman with a landscape plan by Dan Kiley that included extensive community parks and green buffers, the place was almost apparitional in its otherness and, to many in the area, somewhat threatening. Begun in the late '40s, its frank and glassy modernism attracted a particular breed of buyer, educated and liberal (although one must remember that the model liberal government agency in those days was the CIA and we had many neighbor spooks).

This sense of exceptionalism—and beleaguerment—gave the place identity and deepened bonds. There arose both a community of interests and a kind of compensatory communalism that did not exactly derive from spatiality but certainly had it as one of its roots. This sense of shared social, political, recreational interests was continuous with the idea of modernity—and its communal aroma—expressed in the architecture. There was a "sitter's pool" for collectivist baby-sitting, a lively newsletter, a swimming team, collective picnics, amateur theatrics, and organizing for Adlai Stevenson. A feeling of galvanizing otherness was reinforced both by a sense of political isolation in an era when Jim Crow was a local default and by a certain indifference from the organs of local governance. When surrounding roads were running smoothly, snow remained unplowed for days and days in Hollin Hills.

Of course, it was not a halcyon era. In the early days there was a restrictive covenant on deeds that lasted well into the 1950s, when a house was finally sold to a black neurosurgeon. Later Roberta Flack lived down the street. There were many and refined struggles over the dream at the nexus of the formal and the social. A faction that wanted squash courts in addition to the shared tennis courts and swimming pool was spurned for the elitist vibe of the game. Sidewalks were rejected as a denial of the (new) frontier fantasy. And, the design committee that vetted the numerous additions for compliance with the overall architectural tone was not always a source of harmony. On the other hand, the widespread building of additions—and some houses were multiply expanded—was a sign of literal and conceptual investment in the community, and a dedicated and creative response to the fact that many of the houses started small and to the tractability and flexibility of the type. While I don't compare this to other self-help paradigms—like the romanticized squatter settlements that so figured in the thinking of my generation—I do feel that the idea of formal, social, and functional malleability is a key to the prospects for the utility of the suburban.

But let's step back for a minute. Since this has been billed as a debate, I think I am meant to represent the view that there is something irretrievably failed about the suburbs and I'd like to work through the brief for the dark side with which, I must admit, I have some sympathy.

Pure Evil

I am awake—insomniac even—to the possibility that the American suburb is the breeding ground of a terrifying malevolence. When I cruise these places, part of me believes that each basement rec room holds its bound and bleeding JonBenet, that *Fatal Attraction* bunnies boil on every stovetop, that kids contemplating Columbine lurk in the shadows, that spousal abuse in perverse profusion abounds, that George Romero zombies everywhere await the fall of night for their move on the mall. The diffuse and leaky spaces of suburbia, the failures of comfortable enclosure and propinquity, the nonaddictive quality of the strip, the communities gated against a spectral other, all stoke a sinister disquiet. I remember too that during the Cuban missile crisis, when the debate blew about whether one would shoot the neighbor trying to get into the bunker where one's nuclear family was sheltering from the nuclear bomb, the suburbs felt like a homeland of holocaust. Angry at my parents' seeming sangfroid, I went out to the yard and began to dig.

Alienation Factories

Between the mother's little helpers and bowling alone, the suburbs are a petri dish of anomie. We all await the far-too-long-delayed return of *Mad Men*, which is, inter alia, a rumination on suburbia at its high point. Natty admen and their alienated wives drink gallons of martinis to numb the pain of seething meaninglessness. Ties fray and temptations are taken. The routinized behaviors of getting and spending, Little League and PTA, accumulate into a lexicon of nothingness. It is clear that people are unhappy in the suburbs and only a chosen class—men—is liberated to voyage to the fulfillments of the city. Even these, though, are often illusory because the pact of eternally trivial pursuits—and advertising is surely the ultimate expression of the truly empty—has been signed

and signified by that ticket punched to Greenwich every evening, save those when escapist betrayals are consummated in town. Listen up Socrates, the mall is not the agora.

Racism and Regulation

The suburbs were, of course, the destination of white flight, and the dire binarism of sprawl and urban renewal is their expressive morphology. The veterans' benefits that enabled the suburbs' rapid postwar growth were restricted to whites and sealed the bad bargain. That the suburbs effloresced on a rhetoric of freedom and autonomy persuaded tens of millions that that was actually what they were experiencing. This idea that freedom was the reserve for the white chosen also reflexively produced the penal stylings of urban housing projects (let us remember that Athens ran on slavery). The two models had many formal affinities, with a predicate in the idea of single uses, schematically separated: housing in its isolated estate, shopping clumped in dogmatic concision, work at a distance or not at all. And to the monochrome of race were added the exclusions of class. Just as the suburbs were carefully segmented by incomes, so too the architectures of urban renewal were meant to reify the economic isolation of neighborhoods of color. Likewise, the suburban "neighborhood" school was code for segregation and the red-lining of the "slums" served to buttress schools that were deeply deficient in quality, resources, and variety. Interestingly, the post–*Brown v. Board of Education* remedy for the segregated schools of suburbia was the introduction of that quintessentially urban modality: public transportation, in the form of busing.

Here, though, there has been some progress both in the recycling of the inner ring for a far more mixed population and in the slow progress of integrating the middle class itself. At the end of the day, this late buy-in to the historic spatial practice of middle-class America has to be seen as a step forward, as must the reoccupation of the city center by the children of those who had fled.

Distended Infrastructure

A standard-issue critique of the suburbs, but a telling one, is the analysis well made by Myron Orfield, in his classic *Metropolitics*, and by others in the simple proposition that low densities conduce higher infrastructure costs. This is surely true and represents one of the innumerable subsidies that give the lie to the delusion that this pattern somehow embodies the Jeffersonian fantasy of free yeopersons sitting securely in the sustaining increments of property. But here is surely the site in which there is an opportunity for meaningful reform that computes on the sides of both equity and sustainability. The most easily argued logic of densification may not be social (at least in the psychological sense) but economic, a way of more efficiently marshaling resources that are growing more scarce and expensive. That the social life of the street may flourish is a corollary that cements but does not animate the deal.

Creature of the Car

I recently saw a fine film about Victor Gruen, erstwhile father of the shopping mall [*The Gruen Effect: Victor Gruen and the Shopping Mall*, 2009], that was awash with footage of the high-suburban days of the 1960s. The scenes of roads crammed with cars were amazing, mesmerizing, weird. The baroque excesses of the automotive stylings of the time were totally mind-blowing and it's hard to believe that I grew up in the midst of this particular taste culture. For all their charm, these gas-guzzling, unsafe-at-any-speed, what's-good-for-General-Motors behemoths harbinger the death of civilization, the clotting of the planet by a technology that has outgrown its usefulness.

The history of the modern city is fundamentally predicated on a game of catch-up played with movement technologies that were invented with no thought of their impact on the cities they would serve. The industrial city found its form around the demands of the railway, which conduced its vast extension but had dire local consequences: the vast cuttings and yards, the belching smoke, the fire and noise, the other side of the tracks. The same is true of the car, another vehicle for the annihilation of "traditional" urban values—the easy adjacencies, the pleasures and practicalities of the street and its life. Cars *demand* suburbs, the material condition of their easy operation. The automotive system is an efficient distributor for a population living in points fixed and dispersed, but density renders it dysfunctional. The successive scaling-up of the system into trunk roads and highways was never able to keep up and, in its distortions by the compressed diurnal cycle of commuting, only operated against its inner logic as a system designed for an even equilibrium.

Certainly the strategies of suburban redress must include a serious critique of the car and its environmental and human inefficiencies. Ongoing attempts to reconceptualize the suburbs in favor of a pattern of "transit-oriented developments" are surely on the money and, indeed, seek to repattern suburbanism along the lines of one of its originary motivators, the streetcar, itself the victim of a conspiracy of automobile and oil-company collusion. What's good for General Motors and Standard Oil is frankly not good for us. But we should also remain wary of any technologically based magic bullet: high-speed rail is not urbanism.

The Hidden Subsidy

Although the suburbs are bruited as the quintessence of Americanness, an alleged compendium of individual responsibility and resistance to the interventions of the collective, this is a shuck, camouflage for the massive public subsidy that sustains them. It's a typical bit of Republican hypocrisy, the idea that your subsidy is socialism and mine is simply the natural order of things. The suburbs were produced by a variety of handouts, government interventions designed for a dramatic reconfiguration of American space. Low-interest FHA loans, mortgage deductibility, accelerated depreciation on commercial property, direct subsidies for road construction, and the endless dough required to sustain sewers, electric lines, and other infrastructure all provide disproportionate advantage to the pattern of sprawl. Socrates and Glaucon have made similar observations and I do understand that this project seeks to nurture publicity in the field of the private.

Not the Least Green

Again, density and cooperation are the sine qua non of sustainable urban form. In their patterns of distribution, movement, and consumption, the suburbs are an affront to all that is green, despite the camouflage of all that lawn, however xeriscaped. The car truly is the villain of the piece, the enabler of the suburban habit. It is a technology that has run its course, and not simply because it is part of the ozone-depleting, cancer-inducing petrochemical system but because it commands spatial practices that are simply no longer sustainable on a planet of almost 7 billion souls. Compaction and convenience are the quintessence of green urbanism and the car and the suburbs are the enemy.

Festering Swamp of Ill Health and Indolence

The exponential postwar growth of the suburbs correlates precisely with the rise of the televisual system. Indeed, the suburbs represent a kind of cultural and morphological pixilation of their population, a series of bounded monads that collude in producing meanings that always wind up on the one hand as an argument for stasis, and on the other as a series of incitements to consume, to make the system go, through sallies to the mall to stock up on the massively processed provisions that will allow the domestic economy to thrive in its passive, interiorized, couch-spud way.

Our grotesquely obese and afflicted population has been produced not simply by the generally purposeless character of our national culture, and by its appalling disdain for intellectual and other socially beneficial forms of human achievement, but also by the styles of indolence inscribed by the suburban televisual-automotive-consumption apparatus—increasingly the American raison d'être. We are alienated from the body, which becomes a symptom to be cured only by the futile but hugely profitable ministrations of the diet, gym, surgical, fashion, and life-style industries. Does anyone doubt that the reduction of walking to a species of entertainment, the elevation of the tube (and its exponentially growing Web kith) to the absolute default for the intake of information, and the pervasive isolation of suburban life have had a dramatic disembodying impact, that life has become more and more virtual, that we are prisoners in a system that relegates us to farther and farther recesses of a chain of mediation, leaving us ever more remote from the individual bodies and minds of our neighbors?

The Suburb Is Not a City

For a final point, let me intercede with my old drinking buddy from the Hemlock Tavern, Socrates. I've been arguing that the suburbs are *not* a species of the city, however degenerate, but its antithesis. Claims for the idea that they represent a variation might either come from a statistical conceit based on contiguity or, conversely, from the claim that they have, via the putatively nondependent relationships of the edge city, become an autonomous realm. Such arguments, though, slight spatial, political, social, and other *qualitative* descriptions of the city's particularity. While I warmly support the aspirational slogan "Change the dream, change the city," it begs, as an idealist like Socrates would tell you, a fantasy of the good city, a theory of city-ness. For me, the city is a special conduit for the meeting of bodies in space, full of serendipity and friction both. Theories of urban form and density, of modes of movement, of the public realm, are all derivatives of this primary motive. And this is what the suburbs—in their disembodying retreat into monadic privacy—annihilate. Precisely what participants in the *Foreclosed* project must address.

Underneath the lawn, the sidewalk!

In Conclusion

Enough of the riot act! We are gathered today not to lament the afflictions of a set of spatial patterns and practices that have gone wrong but to seek solutions via new logics of sociability, sustainability, and political economy. Much crucial and groundbreaking work has been done and we are increasingly well equipped to offer suggestions for the reform of a pattern gone wrong. Data from the 2010 census, too, reveal that the current pattern of suburban growth is focused on the inner and outer rings, with the "mature" suburbs between them, the suburban *locus classicus*, developing more slowly. The reasons are relatively clear and in some ways encouraging. Reinvigoration of the first ring seems due at once to its friendliness—largely derived from devaluations of aging property—to poorer, more mixed populations and from its proximity to rebounding cities and to public transportation.

At the other end of the scale, the outer, exurban ring has grown at a phenomenal pace, over 25 percent in the past ten years. The reasons lie in development economics—cheaper prices at the periphery—as well as, apparently, in a recapture of the lower densities of the classic suburbs in their early days, still desirable to many who just don't like city life. It appears, too, that the "cost" of these lower prices is greatly reflected in commuting times, the devil's bargain the suburbs have conventionally demanded. From the standpoint of the critique above, this is clearly mixed news and a situation that is differently susceptible to morphological suggestions, save at the largest scale: no amount of gentle prodding or persuasive pro forma is likely to have the effect of an absolutely enforced growth boundary or of differential taxation that would seek to recover the greater public cost of distributed development.

Here is my actual suggestion for those involved in this project: do not limit your proposals to architecture. The forces that created the suburbs included a powerful fantasy of the good life, but it was a life that would have been little achieved without the wide variety of financial, legal, and social institutions that were the practical enablers of this enormous cultural and spatial transformation. We now need to rethink our pattern of settlement at a similar scale, making sure whose dream we're actually advancing. This means thinking way outside the little ticky-tacky box.

An open-studio day was
held on June 18, 2011. It
included presentations
by Michael Bell of Visible
Weather (top row, left
and right, and second
row, left), Andrew Zago
of Zago Architecture (top
row, center, and bottom
row, left), Sam Dufaux of
WORKac (second row,
center, and fourth row,
right), Hilary Sample and
Michael Meredith of
MOS (second row, right—
with Barry Bergdoll to
their left—and fourth
row, center), and Jeanne
Gang of Studio Gang
Architects (third row, left
and bottom row, center).

On June 18, 2011, the *Foreclosed* teams underwent a mid-project critique at MoMA PS1. Each team presented its project to the invited jury, which, in addition to Barry Bergdoll and Reinhold Martin, included Stan Allen, Robert Beyer, Pippo Ciorra, Henry N. Cobb, Laurie Hawkinson, Keith Krumwiede, David Lewis, Damon Rich, Michael Sorkin, Marc Tsurumaki, June Williamson, Mabel Wilson, and Adam Yarinsky. The following fragment has been excerpted from many hours of conversation.

MICHAEL MEREDITH AND HILARY SAMPLE OF
MOS ARCHITECTS
THE ORANGES, NEW JERSEY

MICHAEL MEREDITH
We've been looking at what municipal space essentially is, and have latched onto the streets as the truly municipal space to be developed. Because we're in a transit hub here, we can get rid of much in the way of streets and infrastructure, which are already costing the city quite a bit of money a year. They're not necessary, especially given the density there at the moment; we can densify the street area and have everybody walk and use the commuter hub.

The economic model we're working on with [the economist on our team] Ed Glaeser is a cooperative shared-equity model. In the whole project, one of the things that's interesting for us is the problem of economics, which we're taking very seriously. Even in construction type we've been working with [the engineering firm] AKT on how to get the cost per square foot down to under $100, to see how low we can go and still maintain a high performance value. So we've been looking at different kinds of panelized systems, using concrete sandwich panels to produce for the units a very efficient kit of parts that span something like twelve to fifteen feet. That's quite narrow—just think about the tectonic system of New York City, which is twenty, twenty-five feet, and is based on timber. If you look at an economy of structure and spanning that can produce a more manageable and affordable micro-module for these shared-equity models, you can come up with a kit of parts that allows for the conglomeration or aggregation of these units into larger units.

HILARY SAMPLE
There were several reasons why we selected this site in Orange. For one, Orange is a transit hub, and it has real social problems. Our site is isolated, or segregated in a way, in that the transit station is actually across the highway. One issue is, how do people get there if they want to commute? And another has to do with the fact that these populations are largely immigrants—they're segregated also, in that they don't necessarily have access to education, they're learning to speak English, and so on. This produces a series of different stresses that lead to health issues from obesity to addiction. Some of the

other issues are how to keep this population, rather than displace it, and how to make it denser—that's something we've been talking about with Ed Glaeser.

For inspiration about how to develop a different transit model we're looking to the Vauban development in Freiburg, Germany, a low-car or car-free community that has pushed parking to the corners, the edges, and then has really taken back the idea of the street as a public space. The streets there have become places for kids to play, for people to drop off their groceries, to go home, to shop—the basics of what people need if they are to live in a low-car way in their community. That's about bringing shopping, daycare, and basic necessities back into close proximity with where people work. That leads us to some really radical remassing of the site, but it becomes a way to prioritize.

LAURIE HAWKINSON

This assumption about the connection to Manhattan—the assumption that Manhattan is the primary job source. Where do the people who live in Orange currently work? I presume it's not a majority of them that commutes to Manhattan?

MEREDITH

A lot of people are basically working in the service industries. We've had conversations with Ed about job creation, and if you think about creating a localized infrastructure, one thought is that you're potentially going to produce jobs or income for the people there. The job creation you could produce is still relatively small potatoes in the scheme of things, but if you start to think of infrastructure not on the city or state scale but at a building scale, that starts to change the way you think about maintenance, or about how you'd deal with the community. It's sort of in this cooperative mode.

ADAM YARINSKY

I understand that these concepts are still early in development, but they suggest different attitudes—on the one hand wanting something heroic, a bold move, and on the other something more incremental.

Does each house add a unit of service to an infrastructural net of some kind, electrical, plumbing, etc.? Or is the infrastructure a framework that the house is actually a component of? In other words, do new components link into existing infrastructure, or are you building a big infrastructure that gets subdivided?

MEREDITH

We need to think about this. A series of little plants of sorts would be involved.... We were interested in the aggregation of infrastructure, but it wouldn't happen at just the house-unit scale, because that's probably not practical. It would have to happen within clusters or groups.

YARINSKY

More like community heating power? Something like that?

MEREDITH

Exactly. You'd have to figure out how to integrate it; you could deal with it piece by piece with certain power sources, like solar, but figuring out how to tie all that into a grid to produce a positive energy community—it's not clear yet.

PIPPO CIORRA

I'm a cynical European and I don't know the site, but would your scheme be happening on private land? If so, working on housing is terribly demanding in terms of policy positions and administrations. Working on public spaces and facilities is probably more realistic.

MEREDITH

Part of the interest has to do with the cost of infrastructure in America, and the skewed subsidies that have produced or allowed for the suburbs. Part of our project is a critique of the policies and economic incentives that have produced suburbia, and the damage done because of them. That's why I think the operant idea that large-scale infrastructure can solve everything seems naive in the sense of its actual value and monetary gain.

HENRY N. COBB

I think I'm probably the only person here old enough to have had [the urban planner] Ed Logue as a client. What's interesting to me with these models you have crafted is that Logue's early work in New Haven and Boston was characterized by radical overhaul of infrastructure. Late-career Logue, on the other hand, was characterized by a much more conservative attitude toward infrastructure. You seem to be carrying that into another phase, where you're returning to the boldness of early Logue, but at a micro scale. It's fascinating. That model you've made is fabulous. I wish I understood more about what it really means.

BARRY BERGDOLL

I hear a little ambiguity in your presentation. You begin with a radical proposition that says everyone's going to commute away from here for work anyway, so we don't have to worry about local jobs; we'll just go with the bedroom community. Then you hedge your bets a little and say maybe the infrastructure can supply jobs. At some point your extruded street structures have to have a beginning and an end. There's some sort of relationship to the transit hub, which is going to have a hierarchy. So it seems to me that what you're really talking about is three or four different layers of infrastructure, each of which has to be specified. The highway and the rail line

163

are in there somewhere—what's their relationship to this? How does this system begin and end? I think you have to zoom out and start thinking about the edges of this thing, how it operates as a local network, what it's connecting, and what its effects are on the adjacent neighborhoods.

MEREDITH

The edges should be soft. We want to avoid this becoming a gated community. How we keep the edges unresolved is going to be an interesting negotiation—we're not there yet.

HAWKINSON

Like Harry [Cobb], I was interested in the way you're thinking about infrastructure, and how you would open that term up for us. I think about the real public outside of this, and about what the project means for the individual, and I have a feeling you're talking about something—I know you are—something other than what we traditionally think of as infrastructure. Traditionally, if we can say traditionally, this refers to large-scale infrastructure like highways and transportation, the big stuff. So it's more the real specifics of it that are so interesting, I suppose. I am curious about that.

COBB

I really like the idea of starting with a hypothesis, because it's almost a universal hypothesis. And then seeing what happens when it encounters Main Street and when it encounters a railway station.

JUNE WILLIAMSON

I think that's one of the things that we need to tease out if we're going to use examples like Vauban, which are intentional communities. Part of how they work is people select them, and move there to make alternative choices to the mainstream. If you're seeking to impose this set of alternatives on an already existing population, a nonintentional community, you have to explain how it's all going to work for them. The suburbs are littered with intentional communities—people can choose to live here or there, with a suite of amenities and features that are their life-style choices. How do you navigate that set of narratives with this alternative?

The infrastructure thing—there are lots of precedents out there for micro-infrastructure, for handling things locally before they get into the big system.

SAMPLE

One of the things we're trying to do with respect to infrastructure is switch the economic model of it a little bit. Let's take parking as an example: parking is free in a lot of places, including a lot of the streets here. And it's not free, obviously—as a cost borne by the city, by the

municipality, it's very expensive. We want to take things like that and put the cost back on the people, the user of parking. That then incentivizes people: if they choose to not have a car, they don't have to pay for their parking spot.

On the other hand, take things like heating for housing. That's really a burden for lower-income individuals, and switching it to a more infrastructural model is currently not allowed by city regulations. But if we could have some central plant that served a number of these houses, and then had really efficient building structures, we'd decrease the cost of heating to the individual as well as increase the efficiency of the overall system. Then we could substantially reduce the cost to individuals and put the cost where it belongs, in a sense.

YARINSKY

A few minutes ago, the reaction on your face when someone was referring to retail seemed a little problematic—I was wondering whether you thought about the ability of the residents to shop for basic necessities?

MEREDITH

That might have just been my face [laughter]. No, I think groceries are really important, and that would be part of the development.

HAWKINSON

I suppose the scale question has an architectural implication here, right? There's a question of how large is large, how small is small, and the economics of that.

MEREDITH

I think we're thinking smaller—everything is much smaller. We're interested in how people can afford to live, especially people looking to buy a house right now. The shared-equity model and rent-to-own are two models we've been looking at. A cooperative can work to share equity, so people can save. Let's say a low-income person can go in and purchase a house, or lease it in rent-to-own. This is stuff that's better when the economy starts going, can produce equity, so when they do sell or leave the house, they make money—but it's shared with the cooperative. The cooperative then feels like they have something at stake too: they actually own something. Even though it's a shared ownership, not 100 percent ownership in the traditional American way, in which they can sell it and make money.

DAMON RICH

New Jersey has a remarkably utopian state planning system, which of course is absolutely dysfunctional. But the governor, Chris Christie, in his zeal to make use of whatever's at hand, has convened all kinds of people to talk about how to reform the state planning system. I was in Union City talking about this two weeks ago, and most of the people there who work in the development industry wanted to use it as a tool to smash local zoning codes and insert higher densities. So this might tie in to the question, Who's going to build this? But it also might be, Give them some of your do-gooderism kind of language about the co-ops and what everyone might be getting out with.

MEREDITH

You have to work with a nonprofit developer as opposed to a for-profit developer. When we're starting to do a building, we're probably going to have to work with a nonprofit developer—I would imagine; maybe I'm wrong.

BERGDOLL

When we were doing *Rising Currents*, the verb tense was the future conditional. This project combines the future conditional with the past conditional: What would have happened if the federal stimulus package, following Paul Krugman, had been bigger and sustained and not just a one-shot deal? What would have happened had it been directed in particular ways and had not been subjected to pork-barrel legislation?

MICHAEL BELL OF VISIBLE WEATHER
TEMPLE TERRACE, FLORIDA

MICHAEL BELL

Here's this healthy little city, an incorporated city. We quickly found out that the foreclosure issue as it affects Temple Terrace is really on the perimeter—but on the border of Temple Terrace is greater Tampa, which has a whole different story about foreclosure and risk. To make a long story short, we started to understand that this is a little city, one that considers itself a precinct of historic sanity, inside a bigger city. It's really an enclave of sorts that has tried to wall itself off from Tampa.

It became clear to us that one strategy would be to invite Tampa closer, and try to redefine the edge between them. There's a contentious, fearful, racially charged question about small cities, which we could face by asking that edge not just to absorb the greater population that is projected but to call that population forth. Legally, politically, socially, the small city might be agile enough to do that, to organize an argument. It sounds trivial to put it this way, but when Google acquired YouTube, there was a sense of one powerful company absorbing another in a strategic maneuver. A city as diverse as Tampa or Newark might not be able to act decisively like that. So the small city became a positive thing, and that border became a huge issue.

The city has $715 million a year in aggregate personal income. Its buildings on the tax rolls are worth $1.15 billion. So we started going through that. The goal was to see if we could retroactively claim that the city's $16 million redevelopment project, which has been leveraged into a $300 million project, could do something far greater. The need for housing is far more complex, nuanced, and large than the redevelopment is ever going to provide.

WILLIAMSON

I was taken by this new envisioning of a real estate investment trust [REIT] as a possible vehicle. I think that's another way where you can make an analogy at the level of implementation and development about how things are conventionally done. The REITs haven't even been around all that long, but what they've done is disassociate place and ownership into a collective or corporate model.

BELL

I'm not sure how much we'll stick with this, but the proposal was to invent an REIT that the city of Temple Terrace and its citizens would hold stock in. Aside from the specificity of that, Germany just banned REITs from buying social housing. The Fortress hedge fund in New York bought 48,000 units of Dresden's public housing for $1.25 billion. So a little company with about 200 employees bought an entire city—

WILLIAMSON

—200 employees but a lot of investors.

BELL

—I know, but what spurred Germany to enact the law banning REITs from buying social housing was the disequilibrium between the capacity of leveraged capital in places like New York and London and the paucity of the price for the actual asset, as well as the deterritorializing aspect of REITs.

RICH

Right. And on this there's one thing I don't quite understand: you presented an analysis about what we see in today's suburb being somehow the product of a quite unified and organized financial sector. You're clearly interested in that; I think a lot of us are, and it's an interest of *The Buell Hypothesis*. But why, then, have you focused on structural poetics that either humanize the system, in the same way that people in the Arts and Crafts Movement wanted to, or somehow embody it? Why not use the pedagogical capacities of your architecture to somehow make those financial systems more accessible?

BELL

I completely understand why you're asking that question. It isn't clear here in an easy way yet—maybe it's not clear at all—but in my mind this structure is actually *not* going to be humanizing. What we're pushing for is tension and compression meeting each other in eccentric ways, with processes of torsion that would in fact thwart the seemingly easy flow of the typical suburban condition. It has the house-of-cards character of being barely in balance.

COBB
I think it's fascinating. But my question is what you're going to put before the public in the exhibition. Is it really feasible to present that array? Are you going to condense it somehow, and if so, how?

BELL
Actually, one reason we pursued this many versions of things was to find out ourselves what was possible or not possible architecturally. To be direct, I imagine we will condense it to one proposal that will then go through a whole set of redesign issues. This thirty-three-acre site is essentially operating as one building. As a hypothesis, we wanted to know what could be explored in this area. We also worked on a smaller-scale intervention inculcated with the aspirations of the entire redevelopment. I'm tending toward this smaller one.

STAN ALLEN
Two things really stood out for me. One, you said that the place to work is at the border, the seam between Temple Terrace and Tampa. That got lost in all that other information, but it seemed to me a very powerful insight that has a lot of agency. It would follow from that, also, that the topologies, the densities, don't have to be applied overall.

You also made the point that architects are irrelevant in suburbia because the engineering of low-density housing allows simple plug-ins of the builder housing types. So it has to do with the building industry, with a whole set of expertise that has nothing to do with architecture. But there's a threshold of density in which architects are suddenly necessary. It seems to me that if you could just locate that threshold, explain what the consequences of it would be, then the structural poetics would be in service of a problem, whereas right now they're just up there as a rhetoric.

CIORRA
I don't see a big difference between suburb and nonsuburb today. The problems you've been dealing with are the problems of the contemporary city.

MABEL WILSON
But I just want to tag on to what Stan was saying: part of what I understand this project is doing is analyzing the housing industry, and understanding housing as the production of something. What I found fascinating

about your little statistic was when you said, All they could eke out was x amount of profit from it. That's why architects can't intervene; that's why the intellectual capital of the architect isn't useful, precisely because the profit margin is so small. But what I would love to see is a diagram showing precisely how the production of that particular house happens. The financing, how it's engineered, the materials required, resources, plans—just a simple diagram that shows that it produces x amount of profit, which is why we somehow need to reengineer the production of housing. That could then set up a model for you, and that would be a narrative that I could really understand.

BELL
In 1998 I did a show in Houston called *16 Houses*, with sixteen architects exploring low-income housing. We did a lot of pedagogical work there to explain those kinds of things. So I completely agree. I think a show like this is going to have this double project of explaining itself and also becoming something new. That's something we're all definitely going to have to absorb.

HAWKINSON
I think one thing that's novel in your scheme, and that this site presents, is the opportunity to intervene effectively in the already built-out subdivision morphology of the denser, more mixed node of the project, where you put a few new lots together and put something new inside. But it needs to be represented with that context there, so that its reciprocity with everything around it is clarified.

DAVID LEWIS
My sense is that in doing this kind of cost analysis, the house all of a sudden becomes incredibly transformative, because it both remains familiar and projects forward to something else. Then the analysis becomes a way of engaging people. So I think you have something that is both representational and informational. It has to be understood that it's part of your palette to leverage not only the benefits of the project but also the transformative potential of the exhibition.

JEANNE GANG OF STUDIO GANG ARCHITECTS AND ROBERTA FELDMAN OF STUDIO GANG'S *FORECLOSED* TEAM
CICERO, ILLINOIS

JEANNE GANG
There's a big mismatch between the housing type in Cicero and the new, mainly immigrant residents there: these single-family homes are now housing multiple extended families and relatives. They also don't fit a culture in which outdoor public space is used for festivals,

etc.; there aren't enough spaces for things like that. We know that the new economy that's replacing Cicero's old industries won't be big industry, it's going to be small-scale cottage-type industry. These informal economies could employ a lot of people and make Cicero a vibrant place, but right now there's just no space for that.

So what we've done architecturally is start to think about how to create a system of spaces that would meet people's needs. Those spaces could be purchased, or shares in them could be purchased, just to fit your family. So you might have four living rooms, one bedroom, one kitchen, and a workshop.

CIORRA

But is this the same family that gets this space, or an enlarged or expanded family, or different families in the same building?

GANG

What we've found with people there is, they could have a sister-in-law and her kids living with them. There's a network that's created—they don't have to be immediate family.

WILSON

I wonder if that's a consequence of the fact that the arrow of immigration actually goes both ways. This isn't the dream of assimilation, it's a condition of a transnational identity, where people are constantly moving back and forth. This idea that you would root yourself in a place, and make that investment in it, may not necessarily be the ideal now.

GANG

Right, which is how we got to the concept of expansion and contraction, and allowing people to get more rooms if they need them for however long. The flexibility part of the proposal comes from exactly that point.

ROBERTA FELDMAN

The houses in Cicero are currently about half owner-occupied and then half are investors, absentee landlords. It is indeed a transient population that turns over rapidly.

ROBERT BEYER

So this idea of co-op housing, if that's what it is, in effect has to do with transience. Do you think it works better than rental housing, where people can come and go?

FELDMAN

Ownership is actually a major desire of the population coming up from Latin America, as much as of people from Chicago. The new immigrants may be more flexible in their living arrangements than previous local populations, but home ownership is their key investment. And they believed, frankly, that in the United States the home was a good investment, the best place to put their savings, better than banks. As a result, the foreclosure crisis is just remarkable there, it's so bad.

CIORRA

The big boxes—big buildings, factories—are they active?

GANG

The factory we worked with was foreclosed upon, so we took that as an opportunity to reimagine what would be inside it. We tried to recycle its walls, using them to hold some indoor recreation, some workshops. With a more limited footprint we could do a more vertical deployment of this idea; with more vacant space, a more horizontal one. In general our position is that we're trying to densify the area, and even comparing the more horizontal proposal here to the traditional fabric, we're at 33 percent more density. But we also have both 25 percent more open space and 40 percent more work space.

COBB

That raises an important question about the usefulness of the open space you're proposing versus what exists now. The open space that exists now is attached to the living units. Your open space, it seems to me, is subject to the same critique that modernism's classic towers in the park have been subject to ever since Le Corbusier, which is, yes, there's open space, but who's using it and for what purpose? I'm also confused about the purpose of the ten-story proposal versus the five-story proposal, and what is really driving that?

GANG

We're trying to imagine how you might inhabit an industrial landscape, and testing to different scales. This first, more vertical proposal is to say we have an enclosure that could be a safer place. There's a lot of children in the town now—

FELDMAN

—More than half the population—

GANG

—and the smaller footprint that comes from a more vertical structure gives us an opportunity to create some somewhat protected play areas and fields. Then in the more horizontal idea we were looking at the interface with the existing life of the alleys, which are typical features of Chicago. There are single-family garages that right now aren't really used for cars, they're used for these cottage-industry things that people need, and the cars are all parked out front. So here we were trying to test the relationship between the existing cottage-industry garages and our new, denser housing, which also has bigger scale.

ALLEN
Yes, it seems to me that from the point of view of your social narrative, the most convincing thing is the intervention into the existing bungalow streets, the capturing of that alley space, the notion that one family might own two or even three houses in a row, opening up collective spaces somehow. Which leaves me two thoughts about the other pieces. One is that right now, there are three really separate episodes, right? There's the alley intervention, there's a low-rise, and there's a high-rise. That would be so even if you were to register the lot size of the bungalows more consistently through the project—even if you developed the bungalow, the low-rise, and the high-rise as transformations of one another rather than three separate interventions. Second, the low-rise and the high-rise are made out of the same stuff, right? This is a scheme that's based on the unit, and on different forms of aggregation—there doesn't seem to be a real transformation as you get to the high-rise. Again, that suggests more continuity and blurring of the boundaries of where each intervention begins and ends. Right now the siting seems almost accidental. There seems to be a missed opportunity to weave the whole thing together a little more.

LEWIS
I wonder whether, rather than the oppositional strategy of the big tower and the more dispersed collaboration, you might look at a more graduated set of scales among the larger public spaces arranged through these pieces? Or at a finer-grained exterior or yard, so there's an in-built notion of the yard as a space for the smaller collective family, the expanded cooperative group within the larger public collective?

WILSON
I would argue that the immigrant narrative here is probably radically different from older ones, because we're talking about a global age. The people in Cicero probably identify with their province in Mexico; you might find that part of what their wages are going on is building houses where they are in Mexico. So there's a much more complex, back-and-forth relationship that may not be about planting roots in this place. It actually might provide, not an American Dream, but an Americas Dream. The question of belonging, the notion of emplacement, may need really radical rethinking, because if you did a little ethnographic study of the people of Cicero you would probably find much more complex sets of belongings. Do they belong here? Do they go to Mexico? How often? Are they bringing their families here, and if so, for what reason? I get the sense that your project may be turning up something different about what it means to be rooted in a place.

GANG
Doug Saunders's book *Arrival City* shows that people tend to go back and forth quite a bit in the beginning, but ultimately move to the city. From the rural places, they ultimately become urban. I think our project is really saying that it's time for Cicero to become urban. And mining that further would make it more rich.

COBB
I don't know why I'm having a problem with this, but I'm having a problem. The four diagrams [earlier versions of the diagrams on migration and the Rubik's Cube shown on pp. 96 and 97] are for me the most engaging: in those four we go from an existing tradition to exploring an alternative tradition, and finally you end up with that Rubik's Cube. I find that exploration much more engaging than your tower project at this stage, and more provocative architecturally.

I think one reason is that it doesn't raise all the issues that come out in your piling up of units of different heights and so forth. That introduces a whole range of problematic social, physical, and organizational issues, whereas the Rubik's Cube I find compelling precisely because it's limited to three floors. It's clearly something you can walk through. It clearly hypothesizes a different way of organizing the various elements of housing, in such a way that you preserve the idea of a unit but mix up the different types of rooms in different ways. To me that's very provocative, and the sequence works very well from those diagrams. I'm just really puzzled by what I see as a non sequitur between that and your project, which seems to be struggling to be an architectural statement, but not one that I see as firmly enough connected to the underlying theme somehow. That Rubik's Cube has a resonance with the site; the compaction of it even has a resonance with the industrial history of the site. Everything about it I find exciting, thrilling almost, by comparison with the later evolution of it.

GANG
That's helpful. I think it's clear it's very provocative.

COBB
I just don't get that ten-story cloud rising up there. I understand it as an idea about how you take that foreclosed factory and leave its walls and create a public space and housing from it. But I would challenge you, again: I'm much more interested in how the Rubik's Cube would relate to that somehow.

HAWKINSON
Building on what you're saying and what Michael

Meredith was saying, I think there's a way in which what is described here, in terms of the multigenerational housing and so on, could be the beginning of a narrative of how Americans generally, not just immigrants, are going to be living in the future. Your proposition really challenges the isolation of the single-family house. It may be the introduction of an idea of a family compound or something. You talk about this being globally linked—that term "compound" we associate with living in a part of the world that is alien to us.

MICHAEL SORKIN

You make a valuable generalization about Chicago typology, particularly the alleyways. If the alleyways are conceived of as service spaces, and you have a new idea about postindustrial services, then the way in which they are recuperated for residential use from commerce or agriculture becomes a model that I think has broad applicability and is very challenging in its potential.

SAM DUFAUX OF WORKac
KEIZER, OREGON

Amale Andraos and Dan Wood, partners in WORKac, were unable to attend. Their project was presented by their associate Sam Dufaux and team member Eric Sanderson. At the time of the critique, WORKac's scheme took a very different form from the proposal finally modeled, and involved raising all new streets and buildings above the ground.

SAM DUFAUX

Our site is in Keizer, Oregon. Keizer incorporated as a city in the '80s, becoming its own entity separate from Salem. It's a bedroom community with low taxes, no services, and no mixed use. Currently the city has relatively high unemployment, an aging population, and a high foreclosure rate.

The American Dream is not just about ownership; it's about mobility, education, freedom, stewardship of the land. These are elements of our thinking with this.

LEWIS

How do you anticipate the ground operating from the standpoint of wilderness or natural conditions, given the fact that in order to have all this structure there, you're going to have to be covering it? In other words, it's not to be untouched.

CIORRA

This is not agriculture, it's wilderness.

DUFAUX

It's wilderness, complete wilderness, and it's public land. I think the grid is really what's inhabited by people. We'll

have to design some connections.

LEWIS

But inhabited, say, five meters and above? In other words, how is that cross-cut section actually viable? How do you produce a kind of illusion of wilderness when you've got a highway system and a pretty regulated structure? Was there a tendency to put in place a kind of irony of wilderness?

DUFAUX

The thing about wilderness is that it needs a certain scale to operate. If you have a gradient that's at the level of the land, you just can't liberate it. To have an ecosystem perform at a certain level, it needs to have that size. The grid—its height—is absolutely critical. Because of the changes in geography, it will vary a little. We can imagine that maybe it starts on the ground, maybe at the top of the elevation. That's something we're looking into. Then it would vary depending on the natural topography. The gradient itself would be flat.

HAWKINSON

If it's wild, is it scary? I'm struggling with the differentiation between the surface below and what's above it. Are there bears there?

ERIC SANDERSON

Our notion is that there will be animals moving through, including black bear and elk—migratory species.

HAWKINSON

So it's scary.

DUFAUX

Yeah, but those things, if you behave the right way, don't have to be scary [laughter]. And what you can't see here is that these are forest ecosystems too—it's a Douglas fir forest here, oak savanna over here, and a riparian system going through here.

HAWKINSON

So the height of this project is critical.

SANDERSON

That's right, and we haven't worked that out entirely. We live in mutant ecology. What we're struggling with, and what we're trying to do, is find a way for cities and nature to work together, for the ecology to work and for urban life to work.

ALLEN

I was actually surprised that you returned to that idea and said, "No, it's going to bleed into the streets and be more distributive." It seems to me that if there is this inversion, just go with the island, go with the fortification. Be the fortified human occupation within this slightly challenging natural environment. Don't try to soften it with happy coexistence.

WILSON
I have to add, the narrative of the wilderness is an ideological construct that was actually produced in order to describe America as empty and available for conquest, even though there were people—civilizations—living here. There's a lot of baggage that comes with that image of nature, which is precisely what made the land available for the violence of mining and logging, which in turn produced industrial capital. I think you guys have to unpack that narrative if you want to redeploy it and rescript it and change it to something else.

CIORRA
But it's funny—living in this project, I live in a middle of a wilderness, but if I open my window and look outside, I only see houses. That's interesting.

RICH
I'm curious about the degree of irony with which we're supposed to be receiving these forms, which are super crazy, cartoonish, retro. You do it really well, but it seems a little crazy to be asking you serious questions about this scheme, which just seems clearly so rhetorical. Questioning the tropes that it's based upon, like Mabel was saying, is one thing, but it seems like even that may not be receiving it in the spirit in which it's offered.

DUFAUX
Right, there is definitely a visionary attitude that we're trying to bring in, so I think the rhetoric that goes around it—[laughter].

MARC TSURUMAKI
You could read this as the New Urbanist sits down with the landscape urbanist, and they come up with this sort of idyllic scenario. The landscape runs through, I have my piazza, I face my urban square or circle. So everyone's happy, and that's a reading that's ironic.

DUFAUX
Right, we're looking more into the garden city, in a vertical model.

CIORRA
But separation of levels is such a delicate choice in urbanism. It often produces monsters. So you really have to be careful about that.

LEWIS
I think it's a question of terminology and tone. Really, I'm fascinated by it, but the way it's presented, it creates all this confusion. Is it ironic and satirical, is it visionary and heroic? What is it?

CIORRA
It is visionary. It is provocative.

ANDREW ZAGO OF ZAGO ARCHITECTURE RIALTO, CALIFORNIA

ANDREW ZAGO
We all know California's Inland Empire. It underwent tremendous single-family-home growth through the '80s and '90s and is one of the centers of the foreclosure crisis. To give you an idea of how a lot of the Inland Empire works, if any of you have sat in a window seat flying into LAX, you'll see this landscape of enormous box after enormous box. Those aren't suburbs of Costco; those are distribution centers. From the Port of Los Angeles, everything goes on rails: this is a transfer station for something like 60 percent of the imported goods that come into the United States.

Even though Rialto is far out there, it's to some extent a bedroom community for Los Angeles, and even down in Orange County. Rosena Ranch is a development there, of 1,500 homes. Only a portion, maybe 10 or 15 percent, is done. This is a subdivision that's in deep financial crisis—it basically had a seizure or heart attack in the foreclosure crisis.

What do architects do when faced with a situation like this? Usually, they put on the hat of a planner; they put on the hat of a sociologist. But it seemed to us the question rather is, What can architects do in terms of their core areas of expertise, in form, in space, in program? How can these things affect the public dialogue?

CIORRA
This is a typical aerial photo of suburban America. Who builds this? The developer, and then sells the house? Or is each family building its own house, and you're telling them how to build it?

DAVID BERGMAN
The glib answer is the merchant builder, who's responsible for it anyway—they have a new product to build now. But what's important is the notion of moving away from a monoculture, a monoculture of use and a monoculture of form, which are intertwined. By allowing intersections and divisions of the building footprints, you open up opportunities for multifamily housing, nonresidential programs, units of varying sizes, institutional use. So the footprint of the McMansion can become a community facility, like an elementary school or something along those lines. Then by creating heterogeneity in program and form through these kinds of fiscal moves, we also

intend to create heterogeneity in forms of ownership, and in the structure of regulation. So I would say our amendments or additions to *The Buell Hypothesis* are, Change the subdivision map and you change the city.

ALLEN
I can buy that, and I think your scenario is credible. This is how developers work now on a large-scale subdivision. I assume there'd be a community association that might regulate these things and so on. But a couple of questions about your project and the design of the house transformations: one is, I'm not seeing all the alternatives that you're saying exist there. Instead I see essentially a kind of doubling of the existing house size repeated.

Then, I keep thinking of the opening credits of the TV show *Weeds*, where identically dressed men come out of identical buildings and get into identical Land Rovers. There's an incredibly high degree of regulation in these existing suburbs, so I think to make a convincing argument that you are producing heterogeneity out of a system that presently produces the same thing over and over again, even if it's under the guise of the individual house—

COBB
The misregistration that is so refreshing here has actually morphed into a reregistration, with an implicitly totalitarian presence that makes one wonder. The exercise has turned into something unintended, I think, which is a new registration, instead of what I think is so refreshing, the escape from registration through misregistration. There's a new formal language here that represents a conformism, which is hard to deal with in the context of your thesis.

CIORRA
It's like going to a party where everybody is dressed by the same fashion designer.

WILSON
I just wanted to add, I'm fascinated by the process, but I'm wondering what would happen if you just looked specifically at the way these developers make these homes and the actual variations that occur. If you did a taxonomy of all that stuff to actually understand what that logic is, and then intervene in that, operate within the existing system that's already out there, I'm wondering whether it would produce something far less abstract. I think your methodology is really fascinating, but I do kind of get lost in the abstraction, and I think it's already embedded within the developer logic that you're looking at. That could also be interesting to study on the level of the subdivision's registration, which gets repeated again and again, but at a different scale—that's what you see aerially as you fly across. It isn't just the house, it's also the different subdivisions again and again. I would wonder what happens in those misregistrations between subdivisions as well.

ZAGO
This is our first stab at seeing how it plays out across the landscape. At 2,000 homes or so—with that many, things just start to happen, it becomes regimented and it becomes repetitive. I agree. I think these points are absolutely well taken. We realize that's a problem that we need to work through.

RICH
Maybe one of the things people want to see is, just like animals are allowed to run free, we want to see people running free. When I think about misregistration, I think about people having multigenerational fights over the location of a fence. So to somehow mine those moments, and see what people do with all these canted walls you're proposing—I feel like if there's a tyranny here, it might just be the tyranny of the cant, which just reads as architecture. Which I think is what's covering up the original excitement of the misregistration of the original form.

TSURUMAKI
You're operating at the large scale of the overall subdivision plan, but when we get to the house, I, for one, can't track how the individual operation of each house references the generic plan of the suburban house. I'm wondering if you would take that into the internal logic as well. I think you touched on some of Mabel's points about the conventions that are already embedded within these systems, and how misregistration might operate even on the internal partitioning and contribute to the execution.

SORKIN
Have you actually looked at the plans of these houses? They're really fascinating. There are a lot of freaks out there in suburbia. The generic, I guess for me, is the monopoly house, and I don't think the generic house really exists anymore. But it exists within a range of organizational typologies.

HAWKINSON
That's the thing I'm curious about here. You give people all these different options, but they seem incredibly specific in their application. If you've chosen one and then it no longer suits you somehow, how do you modify?

A final open-studio day was held on September 17, 2011, with a keynote speech by United States Secretary for Housing and Urban Development Shaun Donovan (top row, right; fourth row, center; fifth row, left; and other photos) and live-streamed presentations by Hilary Sample and Michael Meredith of MOS (second row, left), Amale Andraos and Dan Wood of WORKac (fourth row, left), Jeanne Gang of Studio Gang Architects (fourth row, right), Michael Bell of Visible Weather (first row left), and Andrew Zago of Zago Architecture (third from left in second row, right). There was also a panel discussion with Elizabeth Plater-Zyberk (with microphone in fifth row, center) and Moshen Mostafavi (with microphone in third row, left), moderated by Barry Bergdoll and Reinhold Martin (respectively at right and left in third row, left).

From Crisis to Opportunity: Rebuilding Communities in
the Wake of Foreclosure
Shaun Donovan

Shaun Donovan, Secretary of the United States Department of Housing and Urban Development (HUD), was the
keynote speaker after the final day of open-studio events on Saturday, September 17, 2011, at MoMA PS1. Secretary
Donovan took office just a few weeks before the signing of the American Recovery and Reinvestment Act, the point
of departure for *Foreclosed*. His long history of working to provide affordable housing to American families includes
the roles of acting Federal Housing Authority Commissioner in the Clinton/Bush presidential transition and of
Commissioner of New York City's Department of Housing Preservation and Development, from 2004 until he returned to federal administration in 2009. With degrees in both public administration and architecture from Harvard
University, Donovan embodies our conviction of the urgent need for a synthetic relationship between design
research and public policy.

As I listened to the presentations today, I was reminded
of Rahm Emanuel's remark that "you never want a serious crisis to go to waste." And in fact, I think what brings
us together today is an urgent need to use what has
been an absolutely devastating crisis to begin to rethink
our models, not only of homeownership but of neighborhoods and broader settlement patterns across metropolitan areas. I think this is in MoMA's best tradition. As we
think of the social role of art, we think about how often
art takes up undercurrents in our society, things that are
unspoken, unfelt, and it exposes them, provokes us with
them. We have certainly seen artists in local communities
bringing those kinds of issues to the fore in the wake of
a crisis—I think, for instance, of the Life is Art Foundation
in the St. Roch neighborhood of New Orleans, which
exposed so many of the racial and other fault lines in our
society that Katrina bared to the world, or of Axis Alley
in Baltimore—and the work of the five *Foreclosed* teams
is very much in that vein. The particular contribution of
this effort is that it is operating within the context of
challenges in suburban communities that are too often
left undocumented and unexposed. In exposing those
issues to public debate, I hope it will spur significant conversation about these places that are too often forgotten
in our public dialogue.
    But I also think it is more than that, and this is where
the civic nature of architecture as an art, its constructive
sense, comes in. This project is not just about exposing
or provoking but about building toward actual solutions.
What should these places look like? What are the opportunities? How do we begin, if tentatively, to grasp those
opportunities? That ability to reimagine is particularly
exciting to me, and makes me hopeful about the work
that allows us to gather here today.
    I see my role today really as to do three things. First,
to try to knit the specifics of this project into the larger
context of what the country has faced. And I'm going to
attempt to tie it into a historical trend in terms of the way
architects have responded to these types of crisis before.
    Second, I want to talk about some hope for larger
solutions on the federal level that could support the

localized solutions proposed here. I'd hope to create a bridge between federal policy and effort and what can and must be accomplished at the local level, what the federal government cannot and should not attempt to solve on its own or in a single direction.

Then finally I want to challenge all of you to transcend the role that architects and architecture have traditionally played. To be frank, architecture has too often contributed to a cycle of disinvestment and a reemergence of the same kinds of problems of neighborhood decline, often in different form but fundamentally the same cycle. I'd hope we might be part of a more lasting solution to those problems.

So let me begin, first of all, by talking a little about the last time architects were brought to the table to attack a great crisis. That was in the 1960s, the era when the HUD agency was founded. Literally, our cities were burning. And what emerged out of that set of neighborhood and national crises was an engagement on the part of architects with proposals for specific projects for both buildings and neighborhoods. If you travel to the South Bronx, which in many ways represented the epicenter of this crisis—certainly by the late '70s the South Bronx was the symbol of it for the nation—what you see is a series of projects by Richard Meier and others that certainly demonstrated an engagement of architects and architecture with those challenges. It's true that too often that engagement was symbolized by the urban renewal movement, negatively termed by many the "Negro removal movement"; what was often imagined was a set of grand projects that aimed for a tabula rasa, a place to begin anew, without necessarily an engagement with the existing residents, assets, and fabric of those communities. At the same time, though—and here is a very hopeful direction—what emerged was a whole generation of institutional actors in hard-hit poor communities. I would also describe a third sector, then, a group of community-based nonprofits that have grown since that day to become among the most powerful forces in remaking our communities and in the area of affordable housing.

And yet, the engagement of architects in an urban role often worked against those locally based community development corporations. A great example of that is in fact the South Bronx, where during the 1970s, 75 percent of the population fled. My touchstone for that was being an eleven-year-old boy at the World Series at Yankee Stadium, when Howard Cosell—many of you are probably too young to remember Howard Cosell—declared to a national television audience, "Ladies and gentleman, the Bronx is burning." And he had the camera pan out across the outfield and you could see a fire raging across the South Bronx. Two weeks later President Jimmy Carter visited a site right next to Yankee Stadium and compared the neighborhood to Dresden after World War II. Yet the federal efforts to begin rebuilding ultimately came down

to a set of locally based community nonprofits. The one I remember best was the Mid-Bronx Desperadoes, which began to rebuild the very street that Jimmy Carter had visited. But they built it on a model that was essentially Levittown-in-the-South-Bronx: single-family houses on quarter-acre lots. To me this is a perfect frame for how we had a generation of architects engaged in thinking about these neighborhoods, an emerging movement of third-sector nonprofits, and never the twain shall meet.

So to me, the hopefulness about this day, the lesson that I hope we can take from it, is that for us to be productive contributors to this discussion as architects, we must engage with these communities. You've heard me asking a lot of questions about "Who was engaged?" and "How?" and "Who did you speak to?" We must engage as architects in ways that are about the place and its assets, the institutions on the ground, not in an abstract way that reimagines a neighborhood as a tabula rasa. That—and it's no small challenge—is the direction I've tried to engage in at the federal level, because in many ways the federal programs, even up to the beginning of this administration, were stuck in an old model of federal command and control, and lacked the ability to connect to local neighborhoods and neighborhood organizations in a more fundamental way.

With the Recovery Act, though, we began to try to engage in a different way. I particularly want to focus on the Neighborhood Stabilization Program, which has contributed about $7 billion to communities that have been hit by the foreclosure crisis. What Neighborhood Stabilization has done in many communities is provide the tools, the funding, to begin to rebuild housing that has been foreclosed on, and in the process to create jobs. Take Cleveland as an example, where there are 18,000 vacant properties: in communities where Neighborhood Stabilization has focused, we've seen reductions of 40 percent in vacancy rates. The program has also created an opportunity to begin to put in place many of the types of efforts that I see reflected in these projects today. In Cleveland, a series of community groups have engaged with the city on nearly four dozen environmentally sustainable land reuse projects, many of them focusing on urban agriculture and urban greening, and they are coordinated not only with local community groups but with the state university and a range of other partners. One is an organization called the Urban Lumberjacks, who have been removing the most blighted homes in an environmentally sustainable manner, salvaging and recycling materials, while at the same time putting local residents in those communities to work in this deconstruction process. At the larger level, in Cuyahoga County (which surrounds Cleveland) a land bank has been created to begin to own and manage over the long term, and to capture benefits and try to break the cycle of inflation and deflation of values that so hurt families in this crisis. Certainly that connects to a number of projects here that effectively propose land banks as a tool to capture or recapture value in those neighborhoods and dedicate it to a more sustainable vision of wealth creation for those families.

Recognizing these efforts and their importance, as part of the American Jobs Act the president proposed a dramatic expansion of our Neighborhood Stabilization efforts—$15 billion—for what he called Project Rebuild. Specifically that would create a $5 billion competition within that $15 billion. Nonprofits and other local actors would be directly eligible for the funds, which would allow a reimagining of not only devastated inner-city neighborhoods but also suburban communities like the ones that are the subject of the studies here today. That could make possible a very large-scale reimagining, not simply a house-by-house or block-by-block approach. It would also, for the first time, make a broad variety of uses eligible. Neighborhood Stabilization to date has focused only on residential properties; many of the projects here at MoMA PS1, rather than simply focusing on foreclosed homes, rightly involve an integrated vision, whether it's a foreclosed factory, or the need to rebuild infrastructure along with the homes themselves, to use streets and other public infrastructure as a point of departure. All of that would be possible under Project Rebuild.

I want to talk for a moment about the way these projects connect with the surrounding communities. Efforts at a neighborhood scale are only effective to the extent that they connect neighborhoods where foreclosures have been rampant to the broader economy and metropolitan community in which those neighborhoods are embedded. This, I think, is one of the great lessons of the foreclosure crisis. The foreclosure epidemic has been concentrated in the neighborhoods that are the least sustainable in the broadest sense—in places disconnected from transportation, for example, where transportation alternatives like walking or biking are nearly completely unavailable. They're a symptom of the drive-to-qualify culture in our financial and home-ownership system, by which I mean that our affordable housing strategy was effectively, "if you can't afford a home near a job or transportation, just keep driving until you find a home that you can afford, that you can qualify for." And what that has wrought on our metropolitan landscape is exactly what we're here discussing today. Quite simply, we have to construct a financial system that allows us to make investments where transportation and opportunity are connected. We also have to better integrate our thinking about neighborhood-level planning with metropolitan-scale planning.

In that sense I am hopeful that we have begun to see a shift, both at the personal level, in the behavior and desire of the American people, and also, following from

that, a market shift. Today, the average American family spends 52 cents of every dollar they earn on just housing and transportation. This is simply unsustainable. As families spend five times more time commuting than they did a quarter century ago, we've reached a point of unsustainability in terms of personal commuting patterns, and this has begun to reconcentrate families into places better connected to transportation. Our support for that shift is to supply both funding, to allow planning to take place, and expertise, which many communities simply do not have. This is under our Partnership for Sustainable Communities, which brings HUD together with the Department of Transportation and the Environmental Protection Agency and begins for the very first time to allow housing, transportation, and environmental policy to be spoken for with one voice at the federal level.

Another thing that I would say is encouraging on this front is that in many local communities we have begun to see a deep engagement with the arts and with artists. Here I have to mention our partnership with Rocco Landesman at the National Endowment for the Arts, and his "Art Works" effort, which has begun to try to insert the arts as an economic development tool into many communities. In Minnesota, where a light rail line is being built along the University Avenue corridor connecting Minneapolis to St. Paul, 100 artists are working with local businesses and residents to bring their voices to bear. This is critical in terms of not ending up back in the duality that I talked about of architects disconnected from communities. Forty years ago, the insertion of a freeway in that Minnesota community literally tore it apart. Today, artists are working with the community to envision what it would look like restitched together. In Miami, similarly, the ArtPlace partnership is helping the Adrienne Arsht Center for the Performing Arts to develop a largely dormant neighborhood into a new town square, tied to a fast-improving downtown and to the museums and other assets in that community, giving what had been a sprawling region a more concentrated presence.

All of these efforts point to a growing awareness in local and metropolitan governments that the economy of the twenty-first century requires a focus not just on business development—on having the lowest cost of capital or the lowest levels of regulation and taxes—but on the creation of place as an economic development tool. Once, a company could set up shop and expect that labor would follow. But more and more as capital is mobile, businesses are following people rather than the other way around, and place-making is increasingly the way cities and regions are going to attract businesses and economic development. In that sense the projects here are in fact job-creating economic development proposals, not just design proposals.

Finally, let me come back to the challenge to all of you. I began by talking about the cycle of engagement that architects, designers, and MoMA in particular had with the devastation that was visited on so many urban neighborhoods in the 1950s, '60s, and '70s. A result, I think, was not just the urban-renewal failures I've talked about but also, frankly, a retreat on the part of architects and designers from a more engaged view of public policy and the community sphere. I mentioned my own experience, and frankly my disillusionment and frustration with how architects and architecture too often designed in a way that had very little to do with our poorest residents and communities, and were too often disengaged from the broader group of both professionals and residents that the projects here at MoMA PS1 have begun to readdress.

That timidity, that fear of engagement that came out of the difficult lessons of fifty years ago, must be overcome. So what I think is most hopeful about our meeting here today is that this is not simply an isolated event; this is not simply a set of five inspiring efforts that will ultimately fall into the broad ocean of foreclosed properties across this country without broader ripples. My hope is that it is part of a growing reengagement of architects, designers, and artists with the communities that have been so thoroughly devastated by this crisis we've been through; and that we, at the federal level, can be a partner, but only one partner, in that engagement. It must be an engagement that is about listening to communities, understanding what neighborhoods are and what an American dream—or American dreams, rather, given the broad diversity of neighborhoods and peoples that we're talking about—might look like in them, and how we might not impose a vision on those communities but facilitate their reimagining and reenvisioning. That is my firmest and most hopeful thought about this work that I've witnessed today.

Project Credits

MOS
Thoughts on a Walking City
The Oranges, New Jersey

Team leaders
Michael Meredith, Hilary Sample, Principals, MOS.
Team members
Eric Belsky, Joint Center for Housing Studies, Harvard University. Kelly Brownell, Rudd Center of Public Health, Yale University. Ed Glaeser, Department of Economics, Harvard University. Emilie Hagen, Atelier Ten. Chris Reed, Stoss.
MOS
Katy Barkan, Jason Bond, David Delgado, Leigha Dennis, Ian Donnelly, Justin Fowler, Griffin Frazen, Steve Gertner, Fabiana Godoy, Marti Gottsch, Jeremy Keagy, Kate Lisi, Meredith McDaniel, Magdalena Naydekova, Zach Seibold, Mat Staudt, George Valdes. Motion graphics: Philip DiBello. Filmmaker and photographer: Christopher Woebken.

Visible Weather
Simultaneous City
Temple Terrace, Florida

Team leaders
Michael Bell, Eunjeong Seong, Principals, Visible Weather.
Team members
Rosanne Haggerty, Founder and President, Community Solutions. Zachary Kostura, Structural Engineer, Arup. Mark Malekshahi, Associate Principal, Buro Happold. Erik Olsen, Managing Director and CEO, Transsolar Climate Engineering.
Visible Weather
Phillip Crupi, Design Associate. Eunkyoung Kim, Design Associate. Nicholas Chelko, Da Yeon Kim, Eugene Lee, Jovanna Suarez, Stefana Simic.
Transsolar team
Shrikar Bhave, Matthias Rudolph.
Buro Happold team
Joe Mulligan, Ana Serra.
Consultants
Public housing/supportive housing: Peter Hance, City of Bridgeport Housing Authority. Brian Loughlin, Jersey City Housing Authority. Nadine Maleh, Community Solutions. Finance: Jesse M. Keenan, Center for Urban Real Estate, Columbia University. Landscape: Jamie Masyln Larson, Marc Ryan, and Steve Carlucci, West 8.
Thank you
Chaos Group (V-Ray). RenderCore, Highperformance Render Farm. Noa Younse.

Studio Gang
The Garden in the Machine
Cicero, Illinois

Team leader
Jeanne Gang, Principal, Studio Gang Architects.
Team members
Roberta M. Feldman, Director Emeritus, City Design Center, University of Illinois at Chicago, School of Architecture. Theaster Gates, artist, cultural developer, and Founder and Chairman, Rebuild Foundation. Greg Lindsay, journalist and urbanist. Kate Orff, Principal, SCAPE/LANDSCAPE ARCHITECTURE PLLC. Rafi Segal, Principal, Rafi Segal Architecture Urbanism.
Studio Gang Architects
Mark Schendel, Managing Principal; Claire Cahan, Stephen Claeys, William Emmick, Jay Hoffman, Thorsten Johann, Boryana Marcheva, Juan de la Mora, Jeana Ripple, Schuyler Smith, Katrina Stoll, Rolf Temesvari, Rodia Valladares, Weston Walker, Beth Zacherle.
Additional team members
Marlease Bushnell, Gabriel Burkett, Nathan Carley, Hallie Chen, Elizabeth MacWillie, Idan Naor, Jack Schonewolf, Jane Sloss, Landry Smith, Steven Smutney, Charlie Vinz, Evy Zwiebach.
Acknowledgments
Videography: Adam Goss, Red Mike, Chris Murphy, Dean Storm, and Ryan Clark, Spirit of Space. Cicero community: Alejandra Castillo, Ana Godinez, Isidro Gonzalez, Cristine Pope, Guadalupe Sanchez, and Maria Velasquez, Interfaith Leadership Project of Cicero and Berwyn. Cicero Town Hall: Cicero Town President Larry Dominick, Frank Aguilar, Craig Pesek, Cynthia Salvino, Frank Zolp. Water management: Tom Kennedy, Arup. Ecology: Steven Apfelbaum, Applied Ecological Services. Structure: Ron Klemencic, Magnusson Klemencic Associates. Finance: Michael Bodaken, National Housing Trust. Karl Dayson, Community Finance Solutions, University of Salford. Christopher Leinberger, Brookings Institution. Topher L. McDougal, Massachusetts Institute of Technology. Abby Jo Sigal, Enterprise Community Partners. Andy Slettebak, Institute for Community Economics. Transportation: Patricia Casler, Burlington Northern Santa Fe Railway Company. The Hagestad Sandhouse Gang, Northwestern University Transportation Center. Taylor McKinley, Center for Neighborhood Technology. Culture: Alaka Walli, Field Museum Center for Cultural Understanding and Change. Photography: Albert Kahn Associates, Inc., Joseph Lekas Photography. Okrent Associates, Inc.

WORKac
Nature-City
Keizer, Oregon

Team leaders
Amale Andraos and Dan Wood, Principals, WORKac.
Team members
Nature and urbanism: Eric Sanderson, Senior Conservation Ecologist, Wildlife Conservation Society, and Founder and Director, the Welikia Project. John McMorrough, Architecture Program Chair, Taubman College of Architecture and Urban Planning, University of Michigan. Gerald E. Frug, Louis D. Brandeis Professor of Law, Harvard Law School. Infrastructure: Jason Loiselle, Associate, and Laura Kier, Sherwood Design Engineers.
WORK Architecture Company
Sam Dufaux, Patrick Daurio, Marisha Farnsworth, Brantley Highfill, Allan Izzo, Colleen Tuite. Renderings and models: Michael Alexander, Rubèn Carboni, Julcsi Futo, Joanne Hayek, Tamicka Marcy, Brett Masterson, Ian Quate, Deborah Richards, Marcel Sonntag, Neil Wiita, Sarah Witkin. Michael Kennedy, Kennedy Fabrications. Will Pratt, millworker.
Local Keizer expertise
Michael Etzel, architect.
Economics
James F. Lima, James Lima Planning + Development. Alex Stokes, analyst, HR&A Advisors.
Dream experts
Sean McLaughlin, John Parker, Nick Setounski, John Jay, Neal Arthur, Ian Reichenthal, Scott Vitrone, Stuart Smith, and Gary Krieg, Kristen Johnson, Wieden+Kennedy New York. Lena Beug, Moxie Pictures. Adam Robinson, Whitehouse Post. Pancakes (music).

Zago Architecture
Property with Properties
Rialto, California

Team leader
Andrew Zago, Principal, Zago Architecture; Faculty, Southern California Institute of Architecture; and Faculty, University of Illinois Chicago.
Team members
David Bergman, Principal, Metropolitan Research and Economics, and Faculty, Southern California Institute of Architecture. Laura Bouwman, Senior Associate, Zago Architecture. Bruce Danziger, Associate Principal, Arup. Alexander Felson, Director, Urban & Ecological Design Lab, Yale School of Forestry and Environmental Sciences, and Joint Faculty, Yale School of Architecture and School of Forestry and Environmental Sciences.
Zago Architecture
Team: Alysen Hiller, project manager; Maren Allen, Matthew Au, Sarah Blankenbaker, Tyler McMartin, Chris Skeens, Paul Stoelting, Dale Strong. Assistants: Erin Besler, Yu Ping Hsieh, Dong Woo Kim, Yunlong Li, Ana Muñoz, Kai Reaver, Rae Solomon, Ben Warwas, Jingyan Zhang.
Arup team
Eugene de Souza, mechanical engineer. Said Gharbieh, civil/transportation engineer. Anthony Kirby, infrastructure engineer. Jamey Lyzun, mechanical engineer.
Urban & Ecological Design Lab team
James Axley, Jacob Dugopolski, Yoshiki Harada, Alisa May, Nikki Springer, Emily Stevenson, Timothy Terway.
Special consultant
Robert E. Somol, Director, School of Architecture, University of Illinois at Chicago.
Photographer
Joshua White.
Special thanks
Southern California Institute of Architecture (SCI-Arc), Dr. David and Sylvelin Bouwman, Neil Denari, Todd Gannon, The Graham Foundation for Advanced Studies in the Fine Arts, Nancy Grimm, Jeffrey Kipnis, and United States Artists.

Acknowledgments

The *Foreclosed* workshop and exhibition were unusually intense and productive collaborations between many people and organizations at every stage of the project. In addition to those thanked here, leaders and members of the five interdisciplinary teams worked with many people over the course of the workshop and exhibition-planning stages, as evidenced in the Project Credits in this catalogue (p. 180). Similarly, the project was notable for the level of institutional collaboration between The Museum of Modern Art, MoMA PS1, and The Temple Hoyne Buell Center for the Study of American Architecture at Columbia University. We apologize for any oversights in our long roster of thanks.

The research encapsulated in *The Buell Hypothesis* formed the intellectual foundation for the project. We are grateful to the Buell Center, led by its Director, Reinhold Martin, with Program Coordinator Anna Kenoff and Lead Researcher Leah Meisterlin, for this initiative and for their development of such a penetrating body of work. Through all stages of this complex project they generously lent their expertise and time to all aspects of the workshop, exhibition, and publication. They were instrumental in the success of *Foreclosed*.

We wish to thank Glenn D. Lowry, Director, Kathy Halbreich, Associate Director, Klaus Biesenbach, Director of MoMA PS1, and the Trustees of The Museum of Modern Art for their crucial support for the project and for their commitment to institutional experimentation. For financial support our deepest appreciation goes to the funders of the workshop, exhibition, and publication: The Rockefeller Foundation, MoMA's Wallis Annenberg Fund for Innovation in Contemporary Art through the Annenberg Foundation, Andre Singer, and The Richard H. Driehaus Foundation.

While *Foreclosed* is first and foremost a showcase of five architecture teams and the distillation of a curatorial vision, it draws for its impact on the creativity and dedication of MoMA's wealth of exhibition design, graphic, curatorial, and administrative talents. We extend our sincere thanks to Betty Fisher, Production Manager, Department of Exhibition Design and Production; H. Y. Ingrid Chou, Assistant Director, Department of Graphic Design; Margot Weller, Curatorial Assistant, Department of Architecture and Design; and Emma Presler, Department Manager, Department of Architecture and Design, for their singular commitment to this ambitious project.

We are particularly grateful to the leaders of the departments at the Museum and MoMA PS1 who helped make *Foreclosed* happen: James Gara, Chief Operating Officer, and Assistant Treasurer of the Board of Trustees; Patty Lipshutz, General Counsel, and Secretary to the Board of Trustees; Ramona Bannayan, Senior Deputy Director for Exhibitions and Collections; Peter Reed, Senior Deputy Director, Curatorial Affairs; and Michael Margitich, Senior Deputy Director, External Affairs.

We owe thanks to many whose commitment is reflected in this project. At key stages of the process—from selection of team leaders to critiques of work in progress to participations in public debates—members of the selection jury generously volunteered their time and expertise: Klaus Biesenbach; Henry N. Cobb, Founding Partner, Pei Cobb Freed & Partners; Elizabeth Diller, Principal, Diller Scofidio + Renfro; Glenn D. Lowry; Reinhold Martin; Peter Reed; Mark Robbins, Dean, School of Architecture, Syracuse University; June Williamson, Associate Professor, Bernard and Anne Spitzer School of Architecture at City College of New York; and Mabel O. Wilson, Associate Professor, Graduate School of Architecture, Planning and Preservation, Columbia University. We would also like to recognize and thank Stan Allen, Robert Beyer, Keller Easterling, Laurie Hawkinson, Keith Krumweide, David Lewis, Paul Lewis, Damon Rich, Michael Sorkin, Marc Tsurumaki, June Williamson, Mabel Wilson, and Adam Yarinsky for their invaluable participation as jury members for our midterm review.

Colleagues outside the Museum who participated as presenters at public programs raised the bar in vital ways. Thanks go to Ellen Dunham-Jones, Professor of Architecture and Urban Design, Georgia Institute of Architecture, and Michael Sorkin, Distinguished Professor of Architecture and Director of the Graduate Program in Urban Design at the City College of New York, for their presentations at the orientation; and to Mohsen Mostafavi, Dean, Faculty of Design, Harvard Graduate School of Design, Harvard University, and Elizabeth Plater-Zyberk, Principal, Duany Plater-Zyberk & Company, for their commentary on the closing panel discussion. In addition, we appreciate the insight and commentary offered by U.S. Secretary of Housing and Urban Development Shaun Donovan in his keynote address in September at MoMA PS1. We also extend our thanks to those in the U.S. Department of Housing and Urban Development who helped make his involvement possible, including Neill McG. Coleman, General Deputy Assistant Secretary, Office of Public Affairs; Matthew J. Weiner, Senior Speechwriter, Office of Public Affairs; James E. Millikan, Speechwriter, Office of Public Affairs; Alexandra Simbaña, Director of Scheduling; and Ioanna T. Kefalas, Executive Assistant to the Secretary

Both MoMA and MoMA PS1 provided crucial support and guidance for the organization of the workshop-and-exhibition format of the project. At MoMA, we thank Nancy Adelson, Deputy General Counsel; Jan Postma, Chief Financial Officer; Tunji Adeniji, Director, Facilities and Safety; Todd Bishop, Director, Exhibition Funding and MoMA PS1 Development; Maria DeMarco Beardsley, Coordinator of Exhibitions; Christopher Hudson, Publisher, Publications; Kim Mitchell, Chief Communications Officer; Jerry Neuner, Director, Department of Exhibition Design and Production; Stefanii Ruta-Atkins, Head Registrar, Collection Management and Exhibition; Wendy Woon, Deputy

Director for Education; Julia Hoffmann, Creative Director, Advertising and Graphic Design; Julia Kivitz, Associate Director, Finance and Planning; Erik Landsberg, Head, Imaging Services; Lauren Stakias, Associate Director, Exhibition and International Fundraising; Jennifer Cohen, Associate Coordinator, Exhibitions; Jeri Moxley, Manager, Collection and Exhibition Technology; Steven Wheeler, Assistant Registrar; and Rob Jung, Manager, and Sarah Wood, Assistant Manager, Department of Art Handling and Preparation. At MoMA PS1, we thank Peter Katz, Chief Operating Officer; Richard Wilson, Chief of Installation; Rebecca Taylor, Communications Director; Sixto Figueroa, Director of Building Services; Christopher Y. Lew, Assistant Curator; David Figueroa, Head Preparator; Amanda Greene, Manager, Finance and Administration; Zachary Bowman, Visitor Services Assistant Manager and Group Visit Coordinator; Celine Cunha, Staff Accountant; Lizzie Gorfaine, Project Coordinator; Jocelyn Miller, Executive Assistant to the Director; Everett Williams, Graphics Technician; Yun Joo Kang, Former Chief Administrative Officer; Sarah Scandiffio, Former Special Events Manager and Curatorial Assistant for Public Programs; and Anna Dabney Smith, Former Visitor Services Manager. All made significant contributions to ensure the project's success, for which we are grateful.

In MoMA's Department of Publications we extend our gratitude as well to Kara Kirk, Associate Publisher; Marc Sapir, Production Director; David Frankel, Editorial Director; Matthew Pimm, Production Manager; and Hannah Kim, Marketing Coordinator.

In the Department of Architecture and Design we are grateful for the support we enjoyed from the entire staff. In addition to Emma Presler and Margot Weller, we give special thanks to Paul Galloway, Study Center Supervisor; Colin Hartness, Assistant to the Chief Curator; Whitney May, Department Assistant; and interns Matthew Gin and Lily Wong.

Also at the Museum, we extend grateful appreciation to Heidi Speckhart, Development Officer; Elizabeth Burke, Foundation Relations Director; and Mary Jean Melone, Development Associate. Thanks also to Margaret Doyle, Director, Communications; Sarah Jarvis, Publicist; and Kim Donica, Publicity Coordinator. In the Department of Education, special thanks go to Sara Bodinson, Director, Interpretation and Research, and Pablo Helguera, Director, and Laura Beiles Coppola, Assistant Director, Adult and Academic Programs.

We are grateful to MoMA's Department of Information Technology, especially Aaron Lewis, Director, Audio/Visual Services, and Charlie Kalinowski, Howard Deitch, Nathaniel Longcope, Mike Gibbons, Lucas Gonzales, and Bjorn Quenemoen. In the Department of Digital Media, we thank Allegra Burnette, Creative Director, and David Hart, Shannon Darrough, and Dan Phiffer. In the Department of Marketing, our appreciation goes to Rebecca Stokes, Director, Digital Marketing Communications, and Jason Persse, Associate Editor, Development and Membership.

Both the Museum and the Buell Center are very grateful for the support of Mark Wigley, Dean, Columbia Graduate School of Architecture, Planning, and Preservation, as well as the board members of the Temple Hoyne Buell Center for the Study of American Architecture at Columbia University, especially Henry Cobb (Board Chair), Robert Beauregard, Teddy Cruz, Vittoria di Palma, Elizabeth Diller, Dianne Harris, Andreas Huyssen, Mark Jarzombek, Phyllis Lambert, Mabel Wilson, Peter Eisenman (former Board Chair), Thomas Hines (former Board Member), and Marc Treib (former Board Member).

We extend special thanks to those who worked on *The Buell Hypothesis*, including John Barrett, Jordan Carver, Leigha Dennis, Caitlin Hackett, Rachel Hillery, Jake Matatyaou, Mia Pears, Xiao Qin, Mike Robitz, Justine Shapiro-Kline, and Andy Vann. We thank the design teams at MTWTF and Greenblatt-Wexler, including Glen Cummings, Aliza Dzik, Michael Greenblatt, Daniel Koppich, and Jessica Wexler, for their work designing *The Buell Hypothesis*. We would also like to express our appreciation to Glen Cummings, Aliza Dzik, Juan Astasio, and Andrew Shurtz of MTWTF, and to Buell assistants Jordan Carver and Atreyee Ghosh, for their expert work designing and producing this publication.

We also wish to recognize the contributions of the following people inside and outside the Museum, with thanks: Michele Arms, Brett Messenger, Sarah Butler, Claire Corey, James Ewing, Pamela Gunn, Elizabeth Graham, Robert Kastler, Tom Krueger, Maria Marchenkova, and Roberto Rivera.

We extend a special thanks to our colleagues at partner organizations who helped support the project with their generous gifts of time and expertise: Nicholas Anderson, Christopher Beardsley, Rosalie Genevro, Alex Garvin, and Anne Rieselbach.

To all of the above we thank you for an outpouring of vision, invaluable advice, and shared commitment to making university and museum into experimental platforms for the design professions and for our cities and our suburban communities.

Barry Bergdoll
The Philip Johnson Chief Curator,
Department of Architecture and Design

Picture Credits

Michael Bell, Eunjeong Seong: Visible Weather: pp. 17 (fig. 15), 76, 77, 80, 81, 84, 85, 87–89. Jesse Keenan: pp. 78–79.

Jordan Carver on behalf of The Temple Hoyne Buell Center for the Study of American Architecture, Columbia University: p. 13 (fig. 5).

© Duany Plater-Zyberk & Co. Illustrators: Charles Barrett and Manuel Fernandez-Noval: p. 11 (fig. 2).

© 2011 James Ewing, photograph courtesy James Ewing. pp. 58, 64 (top), 66–67 (bottom), 82, 83, 86, 100–101 (top), 102–3, 116, 119, 120 (bottom left and right), 121 (bottom left and right), 124–25 (top), 148, 149, 150 (right).

Jeff Ferzoco, Petra Todorovich, Yoav Hagler for America 2050 at Regional Plan Association: p. 15 (fig. 7).

Fuse: pp. 12–13 (fig. 3).

Map created by Leah Meisterlin with The Temple Hoyne Buell Center for the Study of American Architecture, Columbia University. Data source: U.S. Census Bureau: pp. 48 (fig. 2), 56 (figs. 2–4), 74 (figs. 2–4), 92 (figs. 2–4), 110 (figs. 2–4), 128 (figs. 2–4). Data source: U.S. Census Bureau, analysis by The Temple Hoyne Buell Center for the Study of American Architecture, Columbia University: pp. 49 (fig. 3), 50 (figs. 4–8).

MOS: pp. 16 (fig. 9), 61–63, 64 (bottom), 65, 66–67 (top), 68–71. Photo Christopher Woebken: pp. 16 (fig. 12), 59, 60.

© 2012 The Museum of Modern Art, New York. Photo Thomas Griesel: pp. 14–15 (fig. 6). Photo Brett W. Messenger: pp. 16 (figs. 8, 11), 155. Photo Don Pollard: pp. 16 (fig. 10), 161, 173.

Realty Trac, imagery © 2011 Digital Globe, GeoEye, State of Oregon, U.S. Geological Survey, Terra Metrics, accessed via Google Maps. With additions by The Temple Hoyne Buell Center for the Study of American Architecture, Columbia University: p. 110 (fig. 1).

RealtyTrac, imagery © 2012 Terra Metrics, accessed via Google Maps. With additions by the Temple Hoyne Buell Center for the Study of American Architecture, Columbia University: pp. 56 (fig. 1), 74 (fig. 1), 92 (fig. 1), 128 (fig. 1).

Courtesy Damon Rich and the Queens Museum of Art: p. 18 (fig. 17).

© Time Life Pictures. Courtesy Time & Life Pictures/Getty Images. Photo: Joseph Scherschel: p. 10 (fig. 1).

Studio Gang Architects: pp. 16 (fig. 13), 95, 96 (top), 97 (right), 98 (above and below left), 99 (top), 104–5. Studio Gang Architects and Albert Kahn Associates, Inc.: p. 98 (right). Studio Gang Architects and Joseph Lekas Photography: pp. 94, 106–7. Studio Gang Architects and Spirit of Space: pp. 96–97 (bottom), 99 (bottom), 100–101 (bottom).

Map created by The Temple Hoyne Buell Center for the Study of American Architecture, Columbia University. Data source: "2008 Foreclosure Filings Set Record," USA Today, February 3, 2009: p. 48 (fig. 1). Data source: U.S. Census Bureau: p. 51 (fig. 9).

Courtesy U.S. Geological Survey, Earth Resources Observation and Science (EROS) Center, Sioux Falls, S.Dak. With additions by the Temple Hoyne Buell Center for the Study of American Architecture, Columbia University: pp. 55, 73, 91, 109, 127.

Marc Wanamaker/Bison Archives: p. 12 (fig. 4).

Wieden+Kennedy New York: p. 125 (bottom).

Photo: Joshua White/JWPictures.com: pp. 141 (bottom), 143, 150 (left).

WORKac: pp. 17 (fig. 16), 112–15, 117, 118, 120–21 (top), 122–23.

Zago Architecture: pp. 17 (fig. 14), 130–39, 140–41 (top), 142.

The book cover and flaps include images with the following credits: Michael Bell, Eunjeong Seong: Visible Weather; © 2011 James Ewing, photos courtesy James Ewing; MOS Architects; Studio Gang Architects; photos: Joshua White/JWPictures.com; and Zago Architecture. Full versions of the cover and flap images appear on pp. 58, 63, 64, 70–71, 76, 81, 86, 102–3, 105, 116, 119, 130, 135, 140–41, 143, 148, 149.

182